(ex•ploring)

1. Investigating in a systematic way: examining. 2. Searching into or ranging over for the purpose of discovery.

Getting Started with

Computing Concepts

Mary Anne Poatsy

Linda Lau

Series Created by Dr. Robert T. Grauer

PEARSON

Boston   Columbus   Indianapolis   New York   San Francisco   Upper Saddle River
Amsterdam   Cape Town   Dubai   London   Madrid   Milan   Munich   Paris   Montréal   Toronto
Delhi   Mexico City   São Paulo   Sydney   Hong Kong   Seoul   Singapore   Taipei   Tokyo

Senior Editor: Samantha McAfee Lewis
Team Lead, Project Management: Laura Burgess
Project Manager: Laura Karahalis
Program Manager: Natacha Moore
Development Editor: Barbara Stover
Editorial Assistant: Victoria Lasavath
Director of Product Marketing: Maggie Waples
Director of Field Marketing: Leigh Ann Sims
Field Marketing Managers: Brad Forrester & Joanna Sabella
Marketing Coordinator: Susan Osterlitz

Senior Operations Specialist: Maura Zaldivar
Senior Art Director: Diane Ernsberger
Interior and Cover Design: Diane Ernsberger
Cover Photo: Courtesy of Shutterstock® Images
Associate Director of Design: Blair Brown
Digital Media Editor: Eric Hakanson
Director of Media Development: Taylor Ragan
Media Project Manager, Production: John Cassar
Full-Service Project Management: Jenna Gray, PreMediaGlobal
Composition: PreMediaGlobal

Credits and acknowledgments borrowed from other sources and reproduced, with permission, in this textbook appear on page 51.

Microsoft and/or its respective suppliers make no representations about the suitability of the information contained in the documents and related graphics published as part of the services for any purpose. All such documents and related graphics are provided "as is" without warranty of any kind. Microsoft and/or its respective suppliers hereby disclaim all warranties and conditions with regard to this information, including all warranties and conditions of merchantability, whether express, implied or statutory, fitness for a particular purpose, title and non-infringement. In no event shall Microsoft and/or its respective suppliers be liable for any special, indirect or consequential damages or any damages whatsoever resulting from loss of use, data or profits, whether in an action of contract, negligence or other tortious action, arising out of or in connection with the use or performance of information available from the services.

The documents and related graphics contained herein could include technical inaccuracies or typographical errors. Changes are periodically added to the information herein. Microsoft and/or its respective suppliers may make improvements and/or changes in the product(s) and/or the program(s) described herein at any time. Partial screen shots may be viewed in full within the software version specified.

Microsoft® and Windows® are registered trademarks of the Microsoft Corporation in the U.S.A. and other countries. This book is not sponsored or endorsed by or affiliated with the Microsoft Corporation.

Many of the designations by manufacturers and sellers to distinguish their products are claimed as trademarks. Where those designations appear in this book, and the publisher was aware of a trademark claim, the designations have been printed in initial caps or all caps.

Library of Congress Cataloging-in-Publication Data

Poatsy, Mary Anne.
   Getting started with computing concepts / Mary Anne Poatsy, Linda Lau.—Second edition.
      pages cm
   Includes bibliographical references and index.
   ISBN 978-0-13-343055-4—ISBN 0-13-343055-3
   1. Electronic data processing.   2. Internet.   I. Lau, Linda K., 1958–   II. Title.
   QA76.P57 2015
   004.67'8—dc23

                                    2014001209

10 9 8 7 6 5 4 3 2 1

ISBN-10:   0-13-343055-3
ISBN-13: 978-0-13-343055-4

Dedications

I dedicate this book to my only child, Catherine Shen, who taught me that there is another wonderful life outside of my work. My life has been more fulfilling and exciting with her in it. I also dedicate this book to the loving memory of my dog, Harry, who was by my side, through thick and thin, for 16 years. I miss him dearly, every day.

Linda K. Lau

For my husband Ted, who unselfishly continues to take on more than his share to support me throughout the process; and for my children, Laura, Carolyn, and Teddy, whose encouragement and love have been inspiring.

Mary Anne Poatsy

About the Authors

Dr. Linda K. Lau

Dr. Linda K. Lau joined the faculty of the College of Business and Economics at Longwood University, located in Farmville, Virginia, in 1994. She is currently an Associate Professor of Information Systems and Security (ISYS) with the College. Over the years, Linda had taught many MIS and Management courses, which includes Principles of MIS, Database Management, Systems Analysis and Design, Visual Basic, Introduction to Computer Security, Forensics, and Law, Business Ethics, and Business Statistics. She was honored with the *Outstanding Academic Advisor Award* in 2006. Besides teaching and advising, Linda has authored and co-authored several journal and conference articles, edited two books, and sits on numerous editorial boards. She also serves as the copy editor of the *Journal of Digital Forensics, Security and Law*, which publishes four issues a year. Her current research interest focuses on digital forensics, enterprise resource planning, campus ethics, hybrid/online learning, and e-commerce. She recently completed a computer forensics course on the *X-Ways Integrated Computer Forensics* software.

Linda earned her Ph.D. from Rensselaer Polytechnic Institute in 1993, and her M.B.A. and Bachelor of Science from Illinois State University in 1987 and 1986, respectively. In her younger days, Linda worked as a flight attendant for Singapore International Airlines for six years before coming to America to pursue her academic dream. She also worked as a financial consultant with Salomon Smith Barney from 1999–2000 before returning to the academic world.

Linda resides in Farmville and Richmond with her family.

Mary Anne Poatsy, Series Editor

Mary Anne is a senior faculty member at Montgomery County Community College, teaching various computer applications and concepts courses in face-to-face and online environments. She holds a B.A. in psychology and education from Mount Holyoke College and an M.B.A. in finance from Northwestern University's Kellogg Graduate School of Management.

Mary Anne has more than 12 years of educational experience. She is currently adjunct faculty at Gwynedd-Mercy College and Montgomery County Community College. She has also taught at Bucks County Community College and Muhlenberg College, as well as conducted personal training. Before teaching, she was Vice President at Shearson Lehman in the Municipal Bond Investment Banking Department.

Dr. Robert T. Grauer, Creator of the Exploring Series

Bob Grauer is an Associate Professor in the Department of Computer Information Systems at the University of Miami, where he is a multiple winner of the Outstanding Teaching Award in the School of Business, most recently in 2009. He has written numerous COBOL texts and is the vision behind the Exploring Office series, with more than three million books in print. His work has been translated into three foreign languages and is used in all aspects of higher education at both national and international levels. Bob Grauer has consulted for several major corporations including IBM and American Express. He received his Ph.D. in Operations Research in 1972 from the Polytechnic Institute of Brooklyn.

Contents

Computing Concepts

■ CHAPTER ONE Getting Started with Computing Concepts   1

Acknowledgments

The Exploring team would like to acknowledge and thank all the reviewers who helped us throughout the years by providing us with their invaluable comments, suggestions, and constructive criticism.

We'd like to especially thank our Focus Group attendees and User Diary Reviewers for this edition:

Stephen Z. Jourdan
Auburn University at Montgomery

Ann Rovetto
Horry-Georgetown Technical College

Jacqueline D. Lawson
Henry Ford Community College

Diane L. Smith
Henry Ford Community College

Sven Aelterman
Troy University

Suzanne M. Jeska
County College of Morris

Susan N. Dozier
Tidewater Community College

Robert G. Phipps Jr.
West Virginia University

Mike Michaelson
Palomar College

Mary Beth Tarver
Northwestern State University

Alexandre C. Probst
Colorado Christian University

Phil Nielson
Salt Lake Community College

Carolyn Barren
Macomb Community College

Sue A. McCrory
Missouri State University

Lucy Parakhovnik
California State University, Northridge

Jakie Brown Jr.
Stevenson University

Craig J. Peterson
American InterContinental University

Terry Ray Rigsby
Hill College

Biswadip Ghosh
Metropolitan State University of Denver

Cheryl Sypniewski
Macomb Community College

Lynn Keane
University of South Carolina

Sheila Gionfriddo
Luzerne College

Dick Hewer
Ferris State College

Carolyn Borne
Louisiana State University

Sumathy Chandrashekar
Salisbury University

Laura Marcoulides
Fullerton College

Don Riggs
SUNY Schenectady County Community College

Gary McFall
Purdue University

James Powers
University of Southern Indiana

James Brown
Central Washington University

Brian Powell
West Virginia University

Sherry Lenhart
Terra Community College

Chen Zhang
Bryant University

Nikia Robinson
Indian River State University

Jill Young
Southeast Missouri State University

Debra Hoffman
Southeast Missouri State University

Tommy Lu
Delaware Technical Community College

Mimi Spain
Southern Maine Community College

We'd like to thank everyone who has been involved in reviewing and providing their feedback, including for our previous editions:

Adriana Lumpkin
Midland College

Alan S. Abrahams
Virginia Tech

Ali Berrached
University of Houston–Downtown

Allen Alexander
Delaware Technical & Community College

Andrea Marchese
Maritime College, State University of New York

Andrew Blitz
Broward College; Edison State College

Angel Norman
University of Tennessee, Knoxville

Angela Clark
University of South Alabama

Ann Rovetto
Horry-Georgetown Technical College

Astrid Todd
Guilford Technical Community College

Audrey Gillant
Maritime College, State University of New York

Barbara Stover
Marion Technical College

Barbara Tollinger
Sinclair Community College

Ben Brahim Taha
Auburn University

Beverly Amer
Northern Arizona University

Beverly Fite
Amarillo College

Bonita Volker
Tidewater Community College

Bonnie Homan
San Francisco State University

Brad West
Sinclair Community College

Brian Powell
West Virginia University

Carol Buser
Owens Community College

Carol Roberts
University of Maine

Carolyn Barren
Macomb Community College

Cathy Poyner
Truman State University

Charles Hodgson
Delgado Community College

Cheri Higgins
Illinois State University

Cheryl Hinds
Norfolk State University

Chris Robinson
Northwest State Community College

Cindy Herbert
Metropolitan Community College–Longview

Dana Hooper
University of Alabama

Dana Johnson
North Dakota State University

Daniela Marghitu
Auburn University

David Noel
University of Central Oklahoma

David Pulis
Maritime College, State University of New York

David Thornton
Jacksonville State University

Dawn Medlin
Appalachian State University

Debby Keen
University of Kentucky

Debra Chapman
University of South Alabama

Derrick Huang
Florida Atlantic University

Diana Baran
Henry Ford Community College

Diane Cassidy
The University of North Carolina at Charlotte

Diane Smith
Henry Ford Community College

Don Danner
San Francisco State University

Don Hoggan
Solano College

Doncho Petkov
Eastern Connecticut State University

Donna Ehrhart
State University of New York at Brockport

Elaine Crable
Xavier University

Elizabeth Duett
Delgado Community College

Erhan Uskup
Houston Community College–Northwest

Eric Martin
University of Tennessee

Erika Nadas
Wilbur Wright College

Floyd Winters
Manatee Community College

Frank Lucente
Westmoreland County Community College

G. Jan Wilms
Union University

Gail Cope
Sinclair Community College

Gary DeLorenzo
California University of Pennsylvania

Gary Garrison
Belmont University

George Cassidy
Sussex County Community College

Gerald Braun
Xavier University

Gerald Burgess
Western New Mexico University

Gladys Swindler
Fort Hays State University

Heith Hennel
Valencia Community College

Henry Rudzinski
Central Connecticut State University

Irene Joos
La Roche College

Iwona Rusin
Baker College; Davenport University

J. Roberto Guzman
San Diego Mesa College

Jan Wilms
Union University

Jane Stam
Onondaga Community College

Janet Bringhurst
Utah State University

Jeanette Dix
Ivy Tech Community College

Jennifer Day
Sinclair Community College

Jill Canine
Ivy Tech Community College

Jim Chaffee
The University of Iowa Tippie College of Business

Joanne Lazirko
University of Wisconsin–Milwaukee

Jodi Milliner
Kansas State University

John Hollenbeck
Blue Ridge Community College

John Seydel
Arkansas State University

Judith A. Scheeren
Westmoreland County Community College

Judith Brown
The University of Memphis

Juliana Cypert
Tarrant County College

Kamaljeet Sanghera
George Mason University

Karen Priestly
Northern Virginia Community College

Karen Ravan
Spartanburg Community College

Kathleen Brenan
Ashland University

Ken Busbee
Houston Community College

Kent Foster
Winthrop University

Kevin Anderson
Solano Community College

Kim Wright
The University of Alabama

Kristen Hockman
University of Missouri–Columbia

Kristi Smith
Allegany College of Maryland

Laura McManamon
University of Dayton

Leanne Chun
Leeward Community College

Lee McClain
Western Washington University

Linda D. Collins
Mesa Community College

Linda Johnsonius
Murray State University

Linda Lau
Longwood University

Linda Theus
Jackson State Community College

Linda Williams
Marion Technical College

Lisa Miller
University of Central Oklahoma

Lister Horn
Pensacola Junior College

Lixin Tao
Pace University

Loraine Miller
Cayuga Community College

Lori Kielty
Central Florida Community College

Lorna Wells
Salt Lake Community College

Lorraine Sauchin
Duquesne University

Lucy Parakhovnik (Parker)
California State University, Northridge

Lynn Mancini
Delaware Technical Community College

Mackinzee Escamilla
South Plains College

Marcia Welch
Highline Community College

Margaret McManus
Northwest Florida State College

Margaret Warrick
Allan Hancock College

Marilyn Hibbert
Salt Lake Community College

Mark Choman
Luzerne County Community College

Mary Duncan
University of Missouri–St. Louis

Melissa Nemeth
Indiana University-Purdue University
Indianapolis

Melody Alexander
Ball State University

Michael Douglas
University of Arkansas at Little Rock

Michael Dunklebarger
Alamance Community College

Michael G. Skaff
College of the Sequoias

Michele Budnovitch
Pennsylvania College of Technology

Mike Jochen
East Stroudsburg University

Mike Scroggins
Missouri State University

Muhammed Badamas
Morgan State University

NaLisa Brown
University of the Ozarks

Nancy Grant
Community College of Allegheny
County–South Campus

Nanette Lareau
University of Arkansas Community
College–Morrilton

Pam Brune
Chattanooga State Community College

Pam Uhlenkamp
Iowa Central Community College

Patrick Smith
Marshall Community and Technical College

Paul Addison
Ivy Tech Community College

Paula Ruby
Arkansas State University

Peggy Burrus
Red Rocks Community College

Peter Ross
SUNY Albany

Philip H. Nielson
Salt Lake Community College

Ralph Hooper
University of Alabama

Ranette Halverson
Midwestern State University

Richard Blamer
John Carroll University

Richard Cacace
Pensacola Junior College

Richard Hewer
Ferris State University

Rob Murray
Ivy Tech Community College

Robert Dušek
Northern Virginia Community College

Robert Sindt
Johnson County Community College

Robert Warren
Delgado Community College

Rocky Belcher
Sinclair Community College

Roger Pick
University of Missouri at Kansas City

Ronnie Creel
Troy University

Rosalie Westerberg
Clover Park Technical College

Ruth Neal
Navarro College

Sandra Thomas
Troy University

Sheila Gionfriddo
Luzerne County Community College

Sherrie Geitgey
Northwest State Community College

Sophia Wilberscheid
Indian River State College

Sophie Lee
California State University,
Long Beach

Stacy Johnson
Iowa Central Community College

Stephanie Kramer
Northwest State Community College

Stephen Jourdan
Auburn University Montgomery

Steven Schwarz
Raritan Valley Community College

Sue McCrory
Missouri State University

Susan Fuschetto
Cerritos College

Susan Medlin
UNC Charlotte

Suzan Spitzberg
Oakton Community College

Sven Aelterman
Troy University

Sylvia Brown
Midland College

Tanya Patrick
Clackamas Community College

Terri Holly
Indian River State College

Thomas Rienzo
Western Michigan University

Tina Johnson
Midwestern State University

Tommy Lu
Delaware Technical and Community College

Troy S. Cash
NorthWest Arkansas Community College

Vicki Robertson
Southwest Tennessee Community

Weifeng Chen
California University of Pennsylvania

Wes Anthony
Houston Community College

William Ayen
University of Colorado at Colorado Springs

Wilma Andrews
Virginia Commonwealth University

Yvonne Galusha
University of Iowa

Special thanks to our development and technical team:

Barbara Stover

Cheryl Slavick

Elizabeth Lockley

Heather Hetzler

Jennifer Lynn

Joyce Nielsen

Linda Pogue

Lisa Bucki

Lori Damanti

Mara Zebest

Susan Fry

Preface

The Exploring Series and You

Exploring is Pearson's Office Application series that requires students like you to think "beyond the point and click." In this edition, we have worked to restructure the Exploring experience around the way you, today's modern student, actually use your resources.

The goal of Exploring is, as it has always been, to go further than teaching just the steps to accomplish a task—the series provides the theoretical foundation for you to understand when and why to apply a skill.

As a result, you achieve a deeper understanding of each application and can apply this critical thinking beyond Office and the classroom.

You are practical students, focused on what you need to do to be successful in this course and beyond, and want to be as efficient as possible. Exploring has evolved to meet you where you are and help you achieve success efficiently. Pearson has paid attention to the habits of students today, how you get information, how you are motivated to do well in class, and what your future goals look like. We asked you and your peers for acceptance of new tools we designed to address these points, and you responded with a resounding "YES!"

Here Is What We Learned About You

You are goal-oriented. You want a good grade in this course—so we rethought how Exploring works so that you can learn the how and why behind the skills in this course to be successful now. You also want to be successful in your future career—so we used motivating case studies to show relevance of these skills to your future careers and incorporated Soft Skills, Collaboration, and Analysis Cases in this edition to set you up for success in the future.

You read, prepare, and study differently than students used to. You use textbooks like a tool—you want to easily identify what you need to know and learn it efficiently. We have added key features such as Step Icons, Hands-On Exercise Videos, and tracked everything via page numbers that allow you to navigate the content efficiently, making the concepts accessible and creating a map to success for you to follow.

You go to college now with a different set of skills than students did five years ago. The new edition of Exploring moves you beyond the basics of the software at a faster pace, without sacrificing coverage of the fundamental skills that you need to know. This ensures that you will be engaged from page 1 to the end of the book.

You and your peers have diverse learning styles. With this in mind, we broadened our definition of "student resources" to include Compass, an online skill database; movable Student Reference cards; Hands-On Exercise videos to provide a secondary lecture-like option of review; Soft Skills video exercises to illustrate important non-technical skills; and the most powerful online homework and assessment tool around with a direct 1:1 content match with the Exploring Series, MyITLab. Exploring will be accessible to all students, regardless of learning style.

Providing You with a Map to Success to Move Beyond the Point and Click

All of these changes and additions will provide you with an easy and efficient path to follow to be successful in this course, regardless of your learning style or any existing knowledge you have at the outset. Our goal is to keep you more engaged in both the hands-on and conceptual sides, helping you to achieve a higher level of understanding that will guarantee you success in this course and in your future career. In addition to the vision and experience of the series creator, Robert T. Grauer, we have assembled a tremendously talented team of Office Applications authors who have devoted themselves to teaching you the ins and outs of Microsoft Word, Excel, Access, and PowerPoint. Led in this edition by series editor Mary Anne Poatsy, the whole team is equally dedicated to providing you with a **map to success** to support the Exploring mission of **moving you beyond the point and click**.

Key Features

- **White Pages/Yellow Pages** clearly distinguish the theory (white pages) from the skills covered in the Hands-On Exercises (yellow pages) so students always know what they are supposed to be doing.

- **Enhanced Objective Mapping** enables students to follow a directed path through each chapter, from the objectives list at the chapter opener through the exercises in the end of chapter.
    - **Objectives List:** This provides a simple list of key objectives covered in the chapter. This includes page numbers so students can skip between objectives where they feel they need the most help.
    - **Step Icons:** These icons appear in the white pages and reference the step numbers in the Hands-On Exercises, providing a correlation between the two so students can easily find conceptual help when they are working hands-on and need a refresher.
    - **Quick Concepts Check:** A series of questions that appear briefly at the end of each white page section. These questions cover the most essential concepts in the white pages required for students to be successful in working the Hands-On Exercises. Page numbers are included for easy reference to help students locate the answers.
    - **Chapter Objectives Review:** Appears toward the end of the chapter and reviews all important concepts throughout the chapter. Newly designed in an easy-to-read bulleted format.

- **Key Terms Matching:** A new exercise that requires students to match key terms to their definitions. This requires students to work actively with this important vocabulary and prove conceptual understanding.

- **Case Study** presents a scenario for the chapter, creating a story that ties the Hands-On Exercises together.

- **End-of-Chapter Exercises** offer instructors several options for assessment. Each chapter has approximately 12–15 exercises ranging from multiple choice questions to open-ended projects. Newly included in this is a Key Terms Matching exercise of approximately 20 questions, as well as a Collaboration Case and Soft Skills Case for every chapter.

- **Enhanced Mid-Level Exercises** include a **Creative Case** (for PowerPoint and Word), which allows students some flexibility and creativity, not being bound by a definitive solution, and an **Analysis Case** (for Excel and Access), which requires students to interpret the data they are using to answer an analytic question, as well as **Discover Steps**, which encourage students to use Help or to problem-solve to accomplish a task.

Instructor Resources

The Instructor's Resource Center, available at **www.pearsonhighered.com**, includes the following:

- **Instructor Manual** provides an overview of all available resources as well as student data and solution files for every exercise.

- **Solution Files with Scorecards** assist with grading the Hands-On Exercises and end-of-chapter exercises.

- **Rubrics** for Mid-Level Creative Cases and Beyond the Classroom Cases in Microsoft® Word format enable instructors to customize the assignments for their classes.

- **PowerPoint® Presentations** with notes for each chapter are included for out-of-class study or review.

- **Objectives Lists** map chapter objectives to Hands-On Exercises and end-of-chapter exercises.

- **Multiple Choice and Key Terms Matching Answer Keys**

- **Test Bank** provides objective-based questions for every chapter.

- **Syllabus Templates**

- **Assignment Sheet**

- **File Guide**

Student Resources

Companion Web Site

www.pearsonhighered.com/exploring offers expanded IT resources and self-student tools for students to use for each chapter, including:

- Online Chapter Review

- Glossary

- Chapter Objectives Review

- Web Resources

Getting Started with Computing Concepts

CHAPTER 1

CASE STUDY | Global Volunteer Computer Literacy Program

As a newly recruited Global Volunteer, you are looking forward to your first assignment overseas. For the next six months, you will work in a rural village in the mountainous Guizhou Province, located in the southwestern part of China. Although this is a relatively small village, the residents consist of people from many ethnic backgrounds, speaking many different languages. Because it is surrounded by mountains, this village is also remotely isolated from the rest of the world and has had no proper transportation for centuries. Earlier, Global Volunteers focused on improving the literacy level of the villagers. Now, those villagers who can read will be able to participate in a computer literacy program. With the recent introduction of wireless services to major cities in Guizhou Province, residents of this community can now access the outside world via the Internet. You will help them understand computer technology and use the Internet with ease so that they will be able to reach out to the world and enjoy the benefits of the information superhighway.

Many villagers understand Chinese, with which you are only slightly familiar. Hence, you will not teach the computer literacy classes but will develop a user guide providing a general description of computer concepts—consisting of basic computer terminology, a brief description of the Internet, and information on computer security. Interpreters will translate the user guide into Chinese for use in the computer literacy program. In preparing for your writing assignment, you plan to gather as much information as possible from various sources.

Computer Concepts

As you go through a typical day at work, school, or home, you find computers everywhere—in the office, on campus, at banks, in cybercafés, at bookstores, in department stores, and at gas stations. Perhaps your Business Communications instructor has assigned a group project that you need to access an online database for research, collaborate among team members, and use a word processor to write the final report. Your recent purchases, travel reservations, and membership registrations were most likely completed and processed online. Cell phones, home entertainment, and even the car you drive are dependent on computer technology. You probably don't even realize or stop to think about how often you interact with computers daily because they have become such an important part of your life. Looking forward, computers will continue to play an even more important role in all aspects of your daily life. Therefore, knowing just a bit about how computers operate can make your life much easier, especially when you find it necessary to use them constantly at work, at school, or in the marketplace.

Computers are actually not as complex as many people believe. Although they come in all varieties, sizes, and capabilities, computers are built to input, process, output, and store data and information. *Data* and *information* are terms that are often used interchangeably but actually refer to different things. **Data** are raw facts such as numbers and words that represent people, events, or ideas. These facts are necessary to produce **information**, which are data converted into a usable and meaningful format. For example, a time card is necessary to produce a paycheck. As an hourly employee, a paycheck is much more valuable to you than a time card, but without the time card, it would not be possible to produce the paycheck. A time card is considered data, whereas a paycheck is information. Figure 1 shows the process of transforming data into information. In this section, you will learn about the hardware components of a computer, and how the hardware and software work together to produce the desired output.

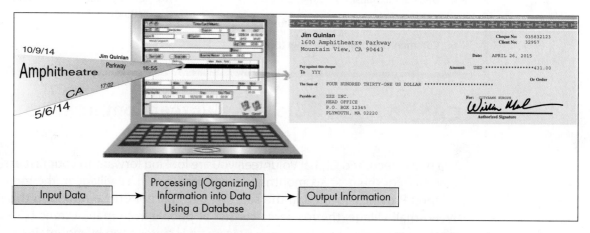

FIGURE 1 Data and Information

Identifying Hardware

When you think of a computer, you basically think of the computer's *hardware* and *software*. **Hardware** comprises tangible pieces of equipment, such as a computer monitor, printer, mouse, and keyboard. However, a discussion of hardware is not possible without mentioning software. The instructions that tell computer hardware how to input data and produce output are called **software**. Without software, a computer simply cannot operate.

Computer hardware is categorized into input, processing, output, and storage devices. Remember that a computer is designed to process data into usable information. It also provides storage for data and information. Specific hardware components are designed for all those tasks. A *keyboard*, *mouse*, and *microphone* provide methods of input, whereas a *monitor*, *speakers*, and *printers* produce output. You can save or store files—such as documents and pictures—on *CDs*, *DVDs*, **hard drives**, or **flash memory** storage devices.

There are two types of software—*system* and *application*. **System software** performs basic computer operations such as accepting keyboard input, saving files, and maintaining system security. Therefore, a computer cannot operate if it is not equipped with system software. You probably enjoy using the Internet to keep up with friends and family, or you might like to create different kinds of documents and work with digital photos. Hence, you also need **application software**, which is any computer program that helps you organize and complete productive tasks at work or school. Software and hardware work hand in hand to enable you to use a computer.

Understand the Different Categories of Computers

There is no clear consensus as to when the first computer was invented; however, most people believe that the first modern computer was developed between 1940 and 1945. Since then, we have evolved through the various generations of computer technology. In general, computers can be classified into one of the following categories.

Supercomputer

Supercomputers are the most powerful systems in the world. Known as the *Cray-1*, the first supercomputer was built in 1976. Although this earlier version had only a few processors, the current models contain massive parallel and multi-core processors. Putting the high price tag aside, supercomputers play an extremely important role in processing a wide range of computationally intensive tasks in fields such as computational science, quantum mechanics, weather forecasting, climate research, oil and gas exploration, molecular modeling, physical simulations, and counter-cryptography. Presently, there are more than 500 supercomputers in the world. Although the fastest supercomputers are located in the United States, Japan, Germany, and China, the rest can be found in countries such as Canada, France, Germany, Italy, Switzerland, Sweden, Norway, the United Kingdom, Spain, Russia, Australia, Saudi Arabia, South Korea, and India.

Mainframe system

Smaller than supercomputers, **mainframes** are large, fast, and powerful computer systems. These machines can have processing speeds that range up to billions of instructions per second. It is quite common for mainframes to possess primary memory consisting of hundreds or thousands of gigabytes. Usage considerations include cost, space, air-conditioning, and uninterrupted power supplies. These systems are frequently used for computations and transactions such as managing airline reservation systems, computing employee payroll, or processing financial transactions in banking institutions. The first mainframe was produced by IBM in 1952, and IBM continues to supply mainframe systems to large corporations today.

Midrange system

Smaller, less powerful, and less expensive than most large mainframe computer systems, but larger, more powerful, and more expensive than most microcomputers, the **midrange computers** are used as high-end workstations for intensive mathematical and engineering computations. Other large-scale processing includes financial institution applications, online analytical processing (OLAP) applications in large Web sites, and integrated enterprise resource planning and manufacturing applications. A significant innovation in the 1960s and 1970s, and more interactive than mainframes, midrange systems are often found in industrial process control systems, such as computer-aided manufacturing (CAM) applications. These computers may also serve as front-end servers to relieve mainframe systems of telecommunications and network management tasks.

Embedded system

A lesser-known category of computers are **embedded systems**, which are developed to perform some specific task, in contrast to the traditional general-purpose computers that are built to perform multiple tasks. Some embedded systems have low or no performance requirements, utilize minimal hardware with little memory, and have a small or nonexistent keyboard or screen, to keep costs to a minimum. The software programs written for embedded systems are stored in read-only memory or flash memory chips. On the other hand, some embedded systems have constraints on real-time performance to meet safety and usability requirements. Embedded systems can be standalone or part of a larger device. An example of an embedded system is the Gibson Robot Guitar, which, besides playing music, has a feature for tuning the strings. Other embedded systems can be found in automobiles and household appliances such as thermostats and refrigerators.

Desktop

The invention of the microprocessor by Intel formed the foundation for *microcomputers*. Also commonly known as *personal computer* or *PC*, **desktop computers** are much smaller than midrange computers in terms of size and capabilities. These personal workstations are usually networked and very popular in the workplace. A desktop computer usually has separate components such as the system unit, keyboard, monitor, and mouse and is intended to remain in one location. The system unit is boxlike, sitting upright or underneath the monitor. However, the **all-in-one desktop** systems can be a good option because of their simple and clutter-free design, which integrates the system unit into a thin, flat-panel monitor, equipped with a high-speed wireless keyboard and mouse (see Figure 2). Other features can include a multi-touchscreen, integrated speakers, webcam, microphone, embedded security, and remote support. If you are evaluating what is the best computer system for your needs, you will need to consider a variety of computing capabilities, physical size, and software selection. You will find that your choice will not be as simple as looking for the fastest machine or the best price.

FIGURE 2 All-in-One Desktop with a Flat-Panel Touchscreen, Wireless Keyboard, and Mouse

Mobile computer

Mobile computers are smaller computers equipped with hardware, software, and communication capabilities to support mobile computing. An option is a *notebook*, which is a self-contained unit, with the monitor, keyboard, system unit, and pointing device all encased together. A notebook, also called a *laptop*, is portable, weighing anywhere from 2 to 12 pounds. A *netbook*, is slightly smaller and lighter than a notebook.

A *tablet* is a mobile computer that is available in various sizes. It usually measures between 7 and 10 inches diagonally. Similar to a desktop or laptop, tablets are equipped with cameras, microphones, touchscreens, and ports for network communications and charging the battery. Tablets do not have a physical keyboard but an on-screen, pop-up virtual keyboard. While tablets in various forms were introduced over time, the iPad was well-embraced by the marketplace and paved the way for wider acceptance of tablets. There is a tremendous increase in the number of Internet users in the United States who use a tablet to read the news, participate in social networking, and watch online video.

Mini tablets are smaller and lighter than their standard counterparts, but they may not have all the features and functions found in the bigger version. Examples of mini tablets include Samsung's 7" Galaxy Tab, Barnes & Noble's Nook Tablet, Blackberry's Playbook, Amazon's Kindle Fire, and Google's Nexus 7. In October 2012, Apple released the 7.9" iPad Mini. Another competitor entering the tablet market is Microsoft's Surface computer, which integrates Microsoft's software with its own hardware.

Phablets, a hybrid between a smartphone and a mini tablet, frequently have a display screen greater than 5 inches. These devices were first released in 2010. Examples of phablets are the LG Optimus Vu, Zync Cloud Z5, Samsung Galaxy Note, and Dell Streak.

Google released its latest invention—*Google Glass*—a wearable computer with an optical head-mounted display (see Figure 3). Weighing only 50 grams, this tiny, wearable computer communicates with the Internet via voice commands through a microphone and displays information to the user in a format similar to a smartphone, but hands-free. Specifications of this new innovation include 16 GB of storage capacity, 1 GB random access memory, prism projector, touchpad, camera, Bluetooth connectivity, and the Android operating system. Google plans to add frames to the lenses and also to explore the possibility of attaching lenses to prescription glasses.[1]

FIGURE 3 A Google Glass Wearable Computer

[1]For more information about the Google Glass, visit http://www.google.com/glass/start/.

Use Input Technologies

Because you will spend much of your time working with a computer, it is important that you learn to identify and work with all different kinds of input devices. Although you most often think of a keyboard and mouse as input devices, you might also use a microphone, a scanner, a digital camera, a touchscreen, and even a stylus pen to input audio, text, or images.

The *keyboard* is a device used to enter data and commands by pressing keys. Keyboard choices are many, both in terms of key arrangement and keyboard type. The *QWERTY* arrangement is the most popular. Named for the first six characters on the top row of letters, it is probably the key arrangement that you learned to use in a keyboarding class or that you see on your computer keyboard. It is not, however, the most efficient arrangement. That honor goes to the *Dvorak* keyboard, which places the most commonly used keys on the home row (middle row). Because your fingers do not have to travel as far when using it, the Dvorak keyboard enables you to produce documents more quickly (assuming that you are adept at using the Dvorak keyboard). Even so, the QWERTY keyboard continues to be preferred, perhaps because of its longevity and the sheer number of people who have learned to use this keyboard. Keyboards used in other countries such as China and Japan may have a set of special keys and a different typing system.

Regardless of key arrangement, keyboards on notebooks are usually more compact than those on desktops. The more compact configuration saves space and weight. Notebook keyboards often assign alternate functions to certain keys so that you get the same capabilities that you would with a full-sized keyboard. You can also attach traditional keyboards to laptops or tablets, or use other specially designed keyboards.

Given the modularity of desktop computer systems, you can easily replace a keyboard with any of a number of keyboard options. A popular choice is an ergonomic keyboard that closely conforms to body structure so that less stress is placed on joints. An additional choice is a wireless keyboard, which is not physically connected to a computer. Wireless keyboards are powered by batteries and send data to a computer through wireless technology. You might even have an interest in a virtual laser keyboard (see Figure 4) that projects the image of a keyboard on any surface. Sensors detect motion as you "type" on the surface, transmitting the appropriate information to the computer.

FIGURE 4 Virtual Laser Keyboard

A *mouse* is a small, handheld device that has buttons that enable you to execute commands, make selections, and open shortcut menus. Invariably, a mouse will be included with any desktop computer and can also be used with notebooks. It can be connected via a cable or work wirelessly. As shown in Figure 5, a wireless mouse does not need to be connected to a computer by a cable, reducing the hassle of having the cable becoming tangled. A wireless mouse uses radio waves to communicate with a computer through a receiver. Whether it is wired or wireless, when you roll the mouse on a flat surface, a corresponding mouse pointer moves on the computer screen.

FIGURE 5 Wireless Mouse

The most popular type of mouse is the *optical mouse*. An **optical mouse** uses a sensor to detect mouse movement, resulting in a corresponding movement of the mouse pointer on the monitor. You will occasionally encounter a mouse with a roller ball on the bottom that detects movement. Dirt and other contaminants can become lodged in the roller ball, making the mouse unusable or necessitating regular cleaning.

Instead of having an external mouse, as found with desktop computer systems, laptops and notebooks commonly include a **touchpad**, a touch-sensitive pad built into the keyboard. By applying slight pressure and dragging a finger over the touchpad, the mouse pointer moves accordingly on the screen. Some touchpads are sensitive to taps, which translate into mouse clicks. A *stylus* (or *stylus pen*) can be used in conjunction with a touchscreen. A **stylus** is a pen-shaped instrument used to input commands to a computer screen or mobile device by drawing, writing, or selecting options on the touchscreen. A **trackpoint**, a small joystick-like device that can be moved with a fingertip, is sometimes included with a laptop or notebook. Figure 6 shows a touchpad and a trackpoint. A notebook keyboard usually includes buttons just beneath the touchpad or trackpoint that you can press to communicate a left- or right-click. If you prefer, you can connect a typical mouse, such as an optical mouse, to a notebook.

FIGURE 6 Touchpad and Trackpoint

With the widespread usage of input devices such as keyboards and mice, it is not surprising that many people develop carpal tunnel syndrome, which is a wrist ailment associated with repeated motion. Those people would probably benefit from using a trackball device, as shown in Figure 7, which minimizes the required wrist movement of using a mouse. The rolling element is on the top or side of the device, so you only move the ball instead of the entire unit. Trackballs are helpful with very young children and anyone else who has limited mobility.

FIGURE 7 Trackball

Most of the time, you will use a mouse or keyboard to enter data or respond to software. Additional input devices, such as a *microphone*, *webcam*, *digital camera*, and *scanner*, enable you to enter data as audio or images. A **microphone** converts sound waves to a digital format for storage on or manipulation by a computer. Mobile computers and smartphones usually have a built-in microphone, but you may connect an external microphone to a desktop computer. Using a microphone, you can record class notes, engage in a teleconference, chat with friends (much like a telephone conversation), and participate in many forms of online audio communication. If you use a computer to make phone calls, you will want to purchase a headset with a built-in microphone. Such a device offers better voice clarity and makes it possible to record high-quality podcasts.

Webcams and **digital cameras** (see Figure 8) collect pictures and video data. Most laptops are equipped with an internal webcam, or you can attach an external webcam to your computer via a universal serial bus (USB) cable. Although you can take photos and videos and save them to your computer, webcams are commonly used for videoconferencing. A digital camera is a camera with a large storage medium, and the photos and videos can be downloaded to a computer via a detachable USB cable or a digital card reader. Using a **scanner**, for instance, the all-in-one unit that includes scanning, printing, copying, and faxing, you can convert existing pictures or text into digital format and send those images to a computer for manipulation and printing.

FIGURE 8 Webcam and Digital Camera

Use Output Technologies

Printing documents, communicating electronically, and playing games are all excellent reasons to use a computer and are all made possible because of output devices. In particular, two primary forms of output—monitor and printer—are components of most computer systems. **Speakers** (for audio output) are also standard computer output devices.

A *monitor* displays text, graphics, and video. The display is called *soft copy* because it is not permanent. That means what you see in one minute will likely change the next. There are three types of monitors being made today—*liquid crystal display (LCD)*, *light-emitting diode (LED)*, and *organic light-emitting diode (OLED)*. An LCD monitor (see Figure 9) is a popular flat-screen display found on notebooks and most new desktop computer systems. A flat-panel LCD does not require much desk space and produces a bright, clear image. The back-lights in LED monitors are brighter than the fluorescent lamps in LCDs and, therefore, can provide a more responsive display. The newer OLED technology provides higher contrast and better viewing angles because it works without a backlight. A disadvantage of the OLED is that it utilizes more power when displaying documents with white or bright backgrounds. Although they are incredibly more expensive than LCDs, OLEDs are becoming more popular in television screens, computer monitors, mobile phones, handheld game consoles, and personal digital assistants.

FIGURE 9 Liquid Crystal Display Monitor

There are several factors that you should consider when selecting a monitor. A monitor's *resolution* is the number of pixels (tiny dots of light, also called picture elements) that are displayed at one time. For example, resolution of 1600 × 1200 means that the display is 1,600 pixels wide and 1,200 pixels high. A higher resolution produces a clearer and sharper image, whereas a lower resolution produces a larger and often more blurred image. The more numerous or tightly packed the pixels, the better the image. Other factors to consider include the viewing angle and the brightness of display.

Tip Change the Resolution

For various reasons, you may want to change your monitor's resolution. For best viewing, some software requires a certain resolution setting. Perhaps you just want to experiment with a different view? To change your monitor's resolution, go to your desktop, right-click an empty area of the desktop, and click Screen resolution. In the Screen Resolution dialog box, click the down arrow beside Resolution. Click, and then drag the resolution slider to adjust the setting. Click Apply if you want to view the new setting and then click Keep changes if you want to use the new setting or click Revert if you want to go back to your original setting. Finally, click OK, or click Cancel to return to the original setting.

A printer produces *hard copy*, which is printed output. Most *printers* are capable of printing both text and color graphics. Printers selected for home use are typically either *ink-jet* or *laser*, as shown in Figure 10. *Inkjet printers* produce high-quality color graphics and documents at an affordable price. Many people use inkjet printers to print color photographs that, with the right paper, rival those of a professional photo printer.

Laser printers, though usually a bit more expensive to purchase than inkjet printers, are increasing in popularity for both home and business users and are typically less costly to operate. Although laser toner cartridges are more expensive, they most often last longer and, therefore, can print more pages than inkjet cartridges. Laser printers typically print faster than inkjet printers too. Laser printers are often shared by multiple computers in classrooms or offices.

Laser printer

Inkjet printer

FIGURE 10 Inkjet and Laser Printers

Other choices for both laser and inkjet printers include *wireless* and *multifunction*. **Wireless printers** most often use either the regular wireless or Bluetooth technology to print from a handheld device such as a smartphone, a notebook computer, or a digital camera. **Multifunction printers** are quite popular, offering the ability to print, scan, copy, and fax—all from one unit (see Figure 11). You can easily buy a multifunction, wireless printer at a very reasonable cost for home use.

FIGURE 11 Multifunction Printer

Speakers enable you to enjoy sound output. You can use speakers to listen to audio, make Internet phone calls, and participate in Web conferencing sessions. Most computers are equipped with inexpensive speakers; however, you can upgrade to more powerful and versatile speakers. You can also easily connect headphones or ear buds to a computer so that you can enjoy audio without disturbing those around you.

Describe the System Unit

Earlier, you learned that a computer is designed to input, process, store, and output information. You have explored hardware that supports input and output activities. The **system unit** handles processing and provides storage—for example, optical drive, hard drive, and solid state drive—so that you can save files and programs for later access. For most desktop computers, the system unit is a large rectangular box. All-in-one computers include the system unit and monitor in one unit. Portable devices such as notebooks and tablets house the system unit in the area beneath and around the keyboard (see Figure 12).

FIGURE 12 System Unit in a Notebook

You can think of the system unit as the control center for your computer. For a desktop unit, the front panel contains power controls as well as one or more **drive bays** for CDs, DVDs, and Blu-ray discs. In addition, you are likely to find ports, which are connectors for peripheral devices such as printers, scanners, mouse devices, flash drives, and **external disk drives**. The most common is the **USB port**, as shown in Figure 13. Because it is such a popular connector, there are usually several USB ports on both the front and the rear panels of the system unit. Other specialized ports are available to connect audio/video devices, microphones, speakers, and monitors.

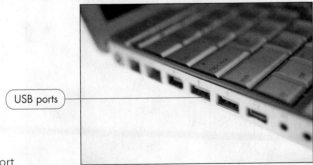

USB ports

FIGURE 13 USB Port

The **central processing unit (CPU)** is a silicon chip (see Figure 14) containing the circuitry that controls all the computer's activities. Also referred to as the *processor*, the CPU is housed inside the system unit on the **motherboard**, which is the main circuit board of a computer. The CPU processes instructions from system memory, also housed on the motherboard. Several factors, including clock speed, the front side bus, the cache, and the number of cores, affect processor performance. A processor's *clock speed* is measured in **gigahertz** (billions of hertz, or electrical vibrations per second). The faster the clock speed, the more quickly the processor executes software instructions. The *front side bus* connects the CPU and system memory, enabling data transfer at a speed that is a percentage of the CPU clock speed. *Cache* is a temporary storage area that enables the CPU to access recently used information very quickly. The size of cache memory, measured in megabytes (discussed later in this chapter), directly affects processor performance. Generally, the larger the cache, the better the CPU performance. Most processors incorporate an *L2* or *L3 cache* with 3 or more MB (megabyte) of easily accessible storage located very near the CPU. Finally, the number of *cores* included on the processor can increase system performance. Predictably, a 2- or 4-core processor (which attaches two or four processors to the same socket) results in more efficient performance and enables simultaneous processing of multiple tasks. Most gaming computers are installed with 8-core or more processors. The motherboard (see Figure 15) also provides space for *random access memory, read-only memory, video cards, sound cards,* and *expansion cards.* A **video card** (video adapter) is a component that provides display capabilities. A **sound card** is a component that enables a computer to work with sound. An **expansion card** is a circuit board that can be connected to the motherboard to give the computer added capabilities. If you are buying a new computer, the configuration of your CPU/random access memory depends on your needs and the processing power that you want from your new machine.

FIGURE 14 Central Processing Unit Chip

FIGURE 15 Motherboard of a Notebook

A computer's memory is referred to as **random access memory (RAM)**. You can compare RAM to a classroom whiteboard. Your instructor can write and erase class notes at will, with the whiteboard contents changing as classes come and go. The whiteboard is *temporary storage*, a term also often applied to RAM. RAM holds programs and data that you are currently working with while your computer is powered on. Because the contents of RAM are erased when your computer is powered off, it is also called *volatile memory*. If you plan to access files and software that you are working with later, you will need to save them to a hard disk or other storage medium.

When you consider purchasing software, you should read the software system requirements. Each software application requires a certain amount of RAM. The amount of memory must be sufficient to accommodate programs that are running simultaneously. The more programs you run at the same time, the larger the demand for RAM. It is common to find at least 8 GB (gigabytes) of RAM in new computer systems. When selecting a computer, purchase as much RAM as you can afford. Later on, if you find that your computer is a little low on RAM, you can most likely add more memory very affordably. Symptoms of insufficient RAM include slow start-up and shutdown; slow processing of large files, particularly, data-intensive Excel or Access files; and slow Internet browsing.

Virtual memory, a standard feature on most desktops and notebooks, frees up space in RAM by transferring data and program instructions that are not immediately needed to an area on the hard disk. When that data is needed, it is transferred into RAM. You will not notice the use of virtual memory because it takes place without any notification or involvement on your part. However, you will notice that you are experiencing insufficient virtual memory when **thrashing** occurs, which is when excessive paging operations take place. Your system will run very slowly and eventually come to a halt. Likewise, application programs cannot distinguish between primary memory (RAM) and virtual memory.

Figure 16 shows a typical bank of RAM. A bank of RAM is a narrow printed circuit board that holds memory chips. Before you decide that your computer is outdated and in need of replacement, check to see if you can upgrade its memory. Because each motherboard is designed to accept only a certain amount and type of RAM, you should review the information on your computer before deciding on a RAM upgrade.

FIGURE 16 Random Access Memory

Tip **View Amount of Random Access Memory**

As you evaluate software that you want to purchase, you will need to make sure that your system has at least the required amount of random access memory (RAM). If you are using Windows operating system, open Settings from the Charms bar, and click PC info.

Read-only memory (ROM), also known as **firmware**, is memory built into the computer that normally can only be read but not written to. ROM is found on the motherboard, along with RAM. Some programs, such as those that accept input from the keyboard or that assist in checking system components when a computer is powered on, are absolutely necessary and should never be erased. Those programs are stored in ROM and cannot be rewritten or modified. Unlike RAM (which is volatile), ROM is *nonvolatile*. That means that its contents are retained, regardless of power supply.

Much like a filing cabinet, disk storage provides a way to save data, files, and software so that you can work with those items later. The internal hard disk drive (see Figure 17), which is found in the system unit, provides a location for permanent storage of software and data. Although you can connect an external hard disk drive (see Figure 17) to a computer, you will most often work with an internal hard disk drive, which simply means that it is installed within the system unit and is not portable. It is important that a computer's hard drive be large enough to support multimedia files as well as software applications, system software, and user files (e.g., documents and worksheets). Most computers come with a terabyte (TB), which is equivalent to a trillion bytes, of hard drive storage. Although that might seem as if it is more than you currently need, you would be well advised to buy as large a hard drive as your budget will allow. A *solid state drive (SSD)* is a primary storage medium residing inside the computer that is built around semiconductors and chips rather than a magnetic media such as the traditional hard drive. This kind of storage is becoming more popular in desktop and mobile computers.

FIGURE 17 Internal and External Hard Disk Drives

Other forms of permanent storage include *CD*, *DVD*, *Blu-ray disc (BD)*, and flash drives. A typical system unit includes one or more of these drives, but usually a DVD drive (called a combo drive, which accommodates both CDs and DVDs). CDs, DVDs, and BDs are considered *optical media* because lasers are used to burn data on the surface of the discs. A DVD-ROM drive reads DVDs, whereas a DVD-RW drive reads and records DVDs and CDs. All optical discs are capable of storing data, music, and video, but a DVD has a much larger capacity (as much as 25 times more than a CD). Figure 18 shows optical discs. BD is a relatively new type of optical storage. Although it resembles a DVD, a BD is capable of storing movies in high-definition (HD) digital format and can hold up to five times more data than a DVD (between 4.5 and 9 hours of HD video). A CD/DVD drive cannot read BDs, but a BD drive can read any type of optical media.

FIGURE 18 Blu-ray Disc and DVD

The most common external storage device is the *flash drive*, or *USB drive* (see Figure 19), a small device that plugs into a USB port. Flash drives are not typically used as primary storage units because they cost much more per unit of storage than a hard drive and are very easy to lose, given their physical size and portability. Instead, most people use a flash drive to move files from one computer to another. You might start a research paper in the classroom and then use a flash drive to take the paper home, where you can work on it on a different computer. Flash drives typically range in capacity from 1 to 512 GB. This type of storage is quite similar to SSD, but SSD is designed to reside inside the computer while a flash drive is an external device. A *memory card* or flash card is another form of flash memory data storage device used to store digital information. They are commonly used in digital cameras, mobile phones, laptop computers, MP3 players, and video game consoles. A card reader—either external or embedded into a device—is necessary to read a memory card.

FIGURE 19 Flash Drive

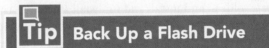

Tip | Back Up a Flash Drive

As tempting as it is, you should never use a flash drive as your primary storage unit because flash drives are small and portable and are also easy to misplace. Make sure that you back up every important file stored on your flash drive on at least one other storage device, such as a hard drive.

With cloud computing technology, the newest form of data storage is online. A few examples of online storage services available free to consumers are OneDrive, Dropbox, and Google Drive. Users can store all kinds of data—text, audio, photos, and videos—on the cloud and can buy additional online storage space from the vendors if needed.

Understand the Binary System

At its most basic level, a computer is designed to work with numbers. The term *computer* suggests a predisposition for calculations and manipulation of numbers. Even the high-quality multimedia video, graphics, and sound experiences enjoyed by today's computer users are all based on a computer's ability to interpret and analyze numeric data. A computer works in a two-state, or *binary*, system, in which circuits must be either "on" or "off." The binary system is described in terms of bits and bytes. A *binary digit (bit)* has two possible values: 0 or 1. Individual bits do not, however, convey meaningful information. Instead, a collection of eight bits, called a *byte*, represents a character. For example, the letter *A* is represented internally as a group of eight bits (0s and 1s), organized in a unique arrangement. Similarly, other characters are represented by unique groups of eight bits.

Every key on a keyboard is represented internally by a series of 0s and 1s. Even audio and video files are converted into the binary system as they are processed by a computer. You do not need to be concerned with precisely how the conversion is accomplished, as you will never have to interpret the internal binary representation to enjoy working with a computer.

So, why should you concern yourself with bits and bytes? As a computer user, you will need to be aware of the size of your computer's memory, as well as the capacity of storage media such as hard disks and flash drives. A computer's memory and storage capacity is expressed in terms of bytes. Such information is important because before you purchase and install new software, you must determine whether your memory and hard disk space are sufficient to meet the software requirements. Because any reference to the size of a computer's memory or the capacity of its disk drives is in terms of bytes, you need to understand the terminology and be able to make informed software purchases.

Working with Software

Software and hardware work hand in hand. The CPU interprets software instructions (or programs) that tell the computer how to accomplish tasks. Software can be classified into two categories: *system* or *application*. Whereas *application software* is concerned with specific user tasks, such as creating documents, sending e-mail, or working with digital photographs, *system software* coordinates communication between the application software and the computer hardware. System software also manages computer resources and keeps a check on the general health of the computer system. System software can be further divided into two groups: the *operating system* and *utility programs*.

Purposes of System Software

For a computer to operate, it must have an operating system. An **operating system** is a program (actually many programs) that allows you to enter data, display text on a monitor, save files to a disk, and print documents. In addition, it makes it possible for you to manage disk space, create folders, and install and uninstall software. An operating system includes security features that create a relatively safe environment in which to communicate electronically. Although it is an extremely important component of a computer system, the operating system is almost transparent, carrying out its work unobtrusively behind the scenes.

Undoubtedly, you are aware of the debate between Windows and Mac operating systems, with some people expressing strong sentiment toward one or the other. Approximately 90% of computers sold today are equipped with a Windows operating system. Produced by Microsoft, the Windows operating system has progressed through many versions. Each improvement in hardware has brought with it a new and better operating system. Windows 8.1 is the latest release that provided improvements in usability and performance. The information in this chapter is written based on Windows 8.1 operating system. OS X Mavericks is the newest Mac operating system, and Linux is also a viable open source operating system used on some computers.

A computer's operating system works in conjunction with the application programs. For example, the operating system coordinates saving your word processing document to a hard disk. It also identifies and reads a memory card from a card reader so that you can use graphics software to modify and print your pictures. These tasks are accomplished with minimal communication with you. Just as you can easily drive a car with very little awareness of the engine dynamics, you can fully enjoy computing tasks with very little interaction with the operating system. However, the more you know about your operating system, the more utility you can get from your computer.

Other mobile digital devices, such as smartphones or tablets, utilize a **mobile operating system**, also referred to as mobile OS, which combines the features of a personal computer operating system with other features. For instance, Apple's iPad, iPhone, and iPod run on iOS. Google products rely on the Android operating system, and Microsoft also has its own Windows mobile OS. However, Android is the only free, open source mobile operating system. The lines of distinction between a mobile OS and a traditional OS are becoming smaller as mobile devices become more powerful and multifunctional.

Another type of system software—**utility programs**—is made up of applications that perform special functions related to coordinating system resources and file management. For example, Optimize Drives is a utility program incorporated into Windows that reorganizes a hard disk for better file access. Security software, such as antivirus, antispyware, and firewall, is included in the utility software category. Compression utilities minimize the size of files for more efficient storage and faster transfer. Even the screen savers that you enjoy are a form of utility software.

Classification of Application Software

Activities such as writing letters, developing financial worksheets, editing photos, creating Web pages, and communicating online are examples of things you can do with application software. In most cases, learning to use application software is simple, requiring just a little effort while delivering a world of enjoyment and productivity.

You will most likely use a computer to create and edit research papers and other documents required in your college classes. Perhaps you are enrolled in a speech class. Your instructor might require that you support your speeches with slideshow presentations prepared on a computer. You could also use a computer to develop a home budget or prepare a flyer for an upcoming event. One category of application software, called *productivity software*, enables you to accomplish all these tasks. Productivity software includes word processing, spreadsheet, database, presentation, and personal information manager (PIM) programs. One of the most widely recognized productivity software suites (collections of programs) is *Microsoft Office Professional*, which includes Word (word processing), Excel (spreadsheets), PowerPoint (presentations), Access (database), Outlook, OneNote, and Publisher. Microsoft Office is available in different versions, with each including various combinations of productivity software. For instance, Office 365 is available online via subscriptions. There are also Web-based programs such as Google Docs and Office Online available online for users to use.

If you enjoy using a camcorder or a digital camera, for instance on your smartphone, you might also be aware of software that enables you to edit pictures, create slideshows, and manage videos. PhotoPad Photo Editor, iPhoto for Mac OS X, iMovie in the iLife suite, Windows Movie Maker, and Windows 8 Photos App are examples of application software that provide support for working with graphics and videos.

 Tip **Get a Free Productivity Software Suite**

Microsoft Office is the leading productivity software suite sold in the United States, but it can be costly to purchase. You can save money by downloading a productivity software suite that is free and enables you to open and work with files that were created in Microsoft Office. Visit www.openoffice.org to explore OpenOffice.org, an open source, Microsoft Office–compatible office suite. Open source software programs are developed and maintained by individuals who have an interest in improving the product. ThinkFree (www.thinkfree.com) is another option for productivity software that is compatible with Microsoft Office. Many Office Online are also available free to Windows users. iApps such as Pages, Numbers, and Keynote are also available for free download to Apple products purchased after October 1, 2013.

When you purchase software (either application or system), or when you subscribe to software packages such as Office 365, you do not own it. You only have the right to use the software within the confines of a software license (user agreement). Often, software developers copyright their work so that making illegal copies violates U.S. copyright law, with stiff penalties for violators. Most software purchased is considered *commercial software*, which means that you are not allowed to copy it. *Shareware*, on the other hand, refers to software that is available as a free trial so that you can download and use it before purchasing. You will find games, screen savers, system utilities, and other programs available as freeware. Some freeware comes with a license agreement, called *copyleft*, which encourages you to adapt and redistribute the software and not restrict future copying. You might wonder why anyone would post a program for free. Sometimes, freeware is the product of a market survey in which your opinion is solicited. Other times, it might be an item that is developed and distributed as part of a graduate project or study. Unfortunately, some freeware might bring with it spyware. It is always a good idea to run anti-spyware software and anti-virus software (discussed later in this chapter) after you have downloaded anything from the Internet.

Computer Networking

Although the concept of the Internet was introduced in 1982, it was not commercialized until 1995. The *Internet* has since become the world's largest network, connecting millions of computers and users around the globe. A *network* makes it possible for computers to interact with one another, sharing files and resources. Because it is so readily available and easy to use, the Internet is an attractive research tool for students and professionals. With its wealth of information, shopping, banking, and entertainment possibilities, you are sure to spend quite a bit of time exploring various Web sites. When you are connected to the Internet, you can purchase almost anything online or download any software applications and games. Colleges and universities offer online courses in many disciplines, making it possible to complete programs of study without physically visiting a college campus. One of the most popular online activities is keeping up with others through social networking sites such as Facebook, Twitter, LinkedIn, Pinterest, Instagram, MySpace, and Tagged. There is no shortage of tasks that can be accomplished online.

Having a home network allows you to share files, peripherals (printers), and an Internet connection and to interact with mobile devices and other devices (smart TVs) in the house. For instance, you can share a printer so that several computers in a house can send documents to the printer. However, all computers accessing the printer must be on the home computer network. In that case, the printer is called a shared printer. Also, in order for all computers to access the printer, it must be turned on, and the computer to which it is connected to must be powered on. The *HomeGroup* feature in Windows 8.1 enables you to easily share a printer. This will be discussed in detail in a later section.

In this section, you will identify the equipment to form a computer network, understand the various methods to transmit data and information, and learn how to share resources and configure a home computer network.

Identifying Network Equipment

There are several ways to connect computers and peripherals together. Computers and peripherals included in a home network can be connected to each other through wired cables (including telephone and electrical wiring) or wireless transmission media. Devices connected in a network, such as computers and peripherals, are called *nodes*. A *wired network* can be built with specialized wiring in the form of coaxial cable or fiber-optic cable and even existing wiring such as phone or power lines. *Wireless networks* use radio waves to communicate between devices. When determining the type of home network to install, you will need to consider the types of computers you are connecting (desktop or notebook) as well as the desired transfer speed and the logistics of your home. Nowadays, most home networks are connected using a combination of wired and wireless technologies.

Each computer and networked device must include a network adapter, which is a device that is connected to (or within) each component to facilitate data transmission. Some network adapters are external, connected to networked equipment through a USB port. *Network interface cards (NIC)* are housed inside the computer on the motherboard. All notebooks and most desktops have *wireless network adapters* built into the motherboards so that they can be connected wirelessly. In addition, USB wireless adapters are inexpensive and widely available. Regardless of how computers and peripherals on a network are connected—wired or wireless—additional hardware in the form of routers, hubs, switches, or adapters are required. For instance, a *router* (see Figure 20) is needed to connect to an Internet modem, enabling several computers to share an Internet connection. Figure 21 shows computers connecting to the Internet through a router and a modem, with a wired or wireless router, and a cable/digital subscriber line (DSL) modem.

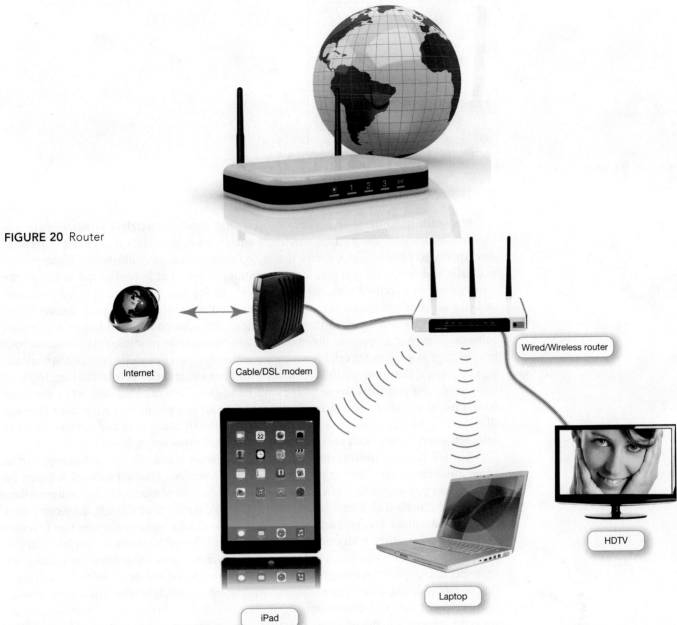

FIGURE 20 Router

FIGURE 21 Home Network

Wireless networks communicate through radio waves. ***Wireless fidelity (Wi-Fi)*** is a technology that uses radio waves to wirelessly transfer data between electronic devices and the Internet. The IEEE (Institute of Electrical and Electronics Engineers) *802.11 standard* (also known as *Wi-Fi*) is the accepted U.S. standard for wireless transfer. It is a family of protocols (methods of communication) that are being developed and used today, with the most common being 802.11g, 802.11n, and 802.11ac (also known as Gigabit Wi-Fi or 5G Wi-Fi). A wireless router broadcasting 802.11n has a longer range than earlier versions; however, unless your home is very large (over 100 yards from end to end), you probably will not notice a difference between 802.11n and earlier versions. Every connected unit (both computer and peripheral, such as a printer) on a wireless network must have a wireless network adapter. One problem with a wireless network is that obstacles such as refrigerators or walls can interfere with wireless signals. Some cordless phones might disrupt communication as well. Wireless networks also have a slower data transfer rate than wired networks, and as distance between units increases, the connection becomes weaker. If you have difficulty communicating between nodes on a wireless network, you might try repositioning the units so that they are closer together. You can also use a ***wireless access point (WAP)***, which is a device that allows other wireless devices to connect to a wired network using Wi-Fi. (see Figure 22). A WAP effectively extends the range of a wireless network.

FIGURE 22 Wireless Access Point

Bluetooth technology—another method that provides wireless communication—uses low-bandwidth, short-range wireless connections (usually less than 30 feet) between computers and peripherals. A device that is equipped with a small Bluetooth chip can automatically and wirelessly transmit data to another device that is configured to accept the transmission in a secured personal area network. In the past, when you updated your contacts list on your cell phone without Bluetooth, you manually entered your contact information and then synchronized that information with your computer using an application software. After you set up your Bluetooth, the synchronization now takes place without your involvement as soon as the cell phone comes within the range of your computer. An advantage of using a Bluetooth-enabled headset with your smartphone is to avoid tangling with any phone cable and you can use your phone hands-free. You can also walk into a store and have a list of all sale items automatically sent to your cell phone or smartphone through Bluetooth technology. Wi-Fi sets up a network between computers and devices with the Internet, whereas Bluetooth provides wireless connections between devices.

A wired network most commonly uses the Ethernet standards and technology, but in some instances, phone lines or powerlines are also used. An *Ethernet network* is based on the Ethernet protocol, which is a set of specifications for wired electronic data transmission. Because Ethernet is such a popular and widely accepted standard worldwide, most computers are designed with an Ethernet adapter (see Figure 23) to which you can connect an Ethernet cable that ties together nodes on your network. An Ethernet network is fast, reliable, and relatively inexpensive compared to other network technologies. Aside from the cabling, the only special equipment required for an Ethernet network is a *hub* or a *switch*. A hub amplifies, or rebroadcasts, data to all connected equipment. A switch is often considered a smart hub, because it not only rebroadcasts signals but also directs them to their intended destination and otherwise manages network traffic. Most routers now have integrated switches or hubs. A separate switch can be easily added to extend the wired capability of a router.

FIGURE 23 Ethernet Adapter and Switch

Another method of connecting a wired network is to use existing home wiring. You might prefer a Home Phoneline Network Alliance (HomePNA) network, which uses existing telephone wiring to connect computers via phone jacks. Another option, *broadband over power line (BPL)*, uses electrical wiring in your home to send information between computers. In both cases, network nodes (computers and peripherals) must be installed with special-purpose adapters to connect to the Internet.

Understanding Transmission Media

A computer must be connected to the Internet before you can do anything online. You have several options, which include *dial-up, cable, digital subscriber line, fiber optics,* and *satellite*. When the Internet was first commercialized in 1995, **dial-up** was the most popular connection type, using existing telephone lines. By today's standards, dial-up connections are painfully slow. Instead, you might consider a *broadband* connection, such as cable, digital subscriber line, fiber optics, or satellite. A **broadband** connection is one that divides a transmission path into channels to accommodate more data traffic. The choice you make depends on how much you are willing to pay for the type of service, the transmission speed you want, and the availability of a signal. Frequently, Web designers assume that most users have broadband connections and include a variety of multimedia components to enrich the online experience. Therefore, to fully enjoy the multimedia resources of the Web, a broadband connection, as opposed to dial-up, is strongly preferred.

Broadband Internet Connections

There are several options of broadband connections to network your computer and peripherals. Two speeds—**upstream** and **downstream** (also known as upload and download speeds)—are very important in broadband. These speeds are measured in **Megabits per second (Mbps)**. The following sections discuss these broadband connections—fiber optics, cable, digital subscriber line, or satellite—in order of popularity.

Connect with fiber optics

Nowadays, the most popular form of transmitting data, voice, and video simultaneously is via the fiber-optic Internet connection, which utilizes a thin glass or plastic strand that transmits data by sending modulated light instead of electricity (see Figure 24). Therefore, unlike copper wire, **fiber optics** is not affected by electrical interference and also has a much higher **bandwidth**—the maximum speed that you can send or receive data. Because the transmission travels at the speed of light, this method of receiving and sending data is extremely fast, which could be as high as 500 MBPS downstream (download speed) and 20 MBPS upstream (upload speed). In fact, a fiber-optic connection can be up to 100 times faster than other broadband connections, such as digital subscriber line or cable. Each fiber-optic line may be shared by many households, so bandwidth may vary depending on competing traffic.

You can expect to pay more for the superfast speed, but for many people the advantages outweigh the cost. Fiber-optic connections are widely used and providers include, but are not limited to, Verizon, AT&T, and Qwest. Unlike digital subscriber line and cable connections that depend on copper wiring that can corrode and experience distance limitations, fiber optics is not limited by distance and seldom disrupted.

FIGURE 24 A Bundle of Fiber Optics

Connect with cable

One of the most popular Internet connections is *cable*, because of its speed and widespread availability. Cable Internet connection is available only if your cable television provider has upgraded existing cable to accommodate two-way communication. You will need a cable modem (see Figure 25) that is connected to your computer so that you can access the Internet. One downside of cable broadband is that the line is shared with others. Therefore, you might notice a decrease in speed during peak usage hours. Many cable companies are very competitive, offering bundling prices if you contract for telephone, television, and computer connections.

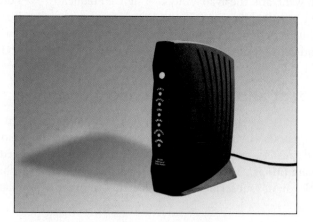

FIGURE 25 Cable Modem

Connect with digital subscriber line

Digital subscriber line (DSL) utilizes high-frequency digital signals over the existing copper voice telephone lines to carry data, voice, and video packages directly from the phone company's switching station into your home. Bandwidth ranges from 1.5 to 6 MBPS downstream but only 64 to 640 KBPS (kilobytes per second) upstream. Service is always available and each home has exclusive use of its line from the house to central office. Computers and other devices connect through Ethernet cable or Wi-Fi using a DSL modem. However, DSL connection is available only if your telephone company has upgraded lines and services to make it possible. You must also be within range of a telephone switching station to take advantage of DSL services. Contact your local telephone company or other companies offering DSL service to see if DSL is an option for you. Although DSL uses existing telephone lines, those lines are divided in such a way that they can carry both data and voice. You will need a DSL modem (see Figure 26) to connect. One advantage of using DSL over cable is that you do not share the line with other users in your area, so you are less likely to notice fluctuations in transmission speed. However, the connection deteriorates the further it travels from the phone company's central office and has a maximum range of 3 miles. People living closer to a switching station will have more efficient service than those at the other end.

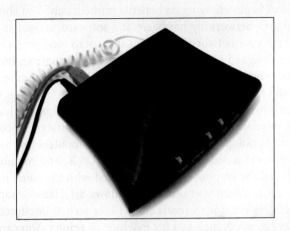

FIGURE 26 Digital Subscriber Line Modem

In part, the speed of a DSL connection depends on the plan in your contract. More than likely your phone company will act as your DSL provider because it owns the wiring used to provide service. DSL typically provides asynchronous access, meaning that the time it takes to transfer files from your computer to the Internet is slower than that required to get files from the Internet.

Connect with satellite

If you live in an area where fiber-optic, DSL, and cable connections are not possible, you could consider connecting to the Internet through *satellite* technology. Satellites are constantly orbiting the earth, so almost anyone in the world can receive satellite transmission. The special equipment required is a satellite dish placed outside (facing south, if you live in North America), which is then connected to your computer by cable. Although satellite transmission is considered broadband, it can be slower than other broadband connections. Because the transmission is not wired, it is possible for air interference and poor weather conditions to disrupt communication. Also, high buildings, mountains, and other objects can block a satellite signal. Despite these disadvantages, satellite is an appealing option to those who are not candidates for other broadband connections and who are not willing to settle for dial-up's even slower speed.

Dial-Up Internet Connection

Dial-up connection is the oldest technology that uses your home telephone line to link your computer to the Internet and is quickly becoming obsolete. Compared to broadband, dial-up is very slow. Before Web pages were designed with rich multimedia content, dial-up was slow but sufficient. However, because of multimedia content, most Web pages typically load on your screen at a creeping pace with a dial-up connection, making it impossible to enjoy the rich resources of the Web. In addition, when the phone line is shared with the Internet connection, you cannot make or receive phone calls while you are connected to the Internet with dial-up. The only advantage of using dial-up is its low price—nothing more than what you pay for a telephone hookup and a small monthly fee to an Internet service provider (ISP). However, most people agree that the low cost does not outweigh the disadvantages. Dial-up is an attractive option only for people who are not within range of a broadband connection or who place great value on the low cost.

Configuring a Home Network

Computers in the computer lab at your school likely share the same printer. You may be able to access a common drive at work so that you and your coworkers can easily share files and software. Similarly, it is very helpful to have a home computer network that all computers in your household can use to share a printer or access the Internet simultaneously. Home networks are neither overly complicated nor costly. If you moved into your own apartment recently, you can set up your own computer network with only a little bit of skill and confidence and begin enjoying its benefits immediately. You should, however, have some basic knowledge of networking hardware and software, as well as an understanding of what you expect from your network before you attempt to configure a home network. Most home networks are designed so that several computers can share an Internet connection and a printer. Some home networks also share a hard drive or are configured so that you can transfer information and files between computers.

After physically connecting all computer equipment included in a network (wired or wireless, or some combination), you must use software to configure the network and share resources. Although a network can include computers that are running different versions of operating systems, such as Windows, Mac OS X, and mobile operating systems, it is much simpler if all the computers are configured with the same operating system—for instance, Windows 8.1. When you use the Windows 8.1 *HomeGroup* feature, all computers in the home network are able to access shared files such as document libraries, music, and pictures and other resources such as a fax machine or printer. You can password protect the network so that only users with access to the password can connect to the network. Also, each computer user can decide which files to share and at what level. For instance, files saved as read-only can be read but not edited or deleted.

A computer with any version of Windows 8 can join a homegroup. However, only those running Windows 8 or Windows 8.1 Home Premium, Professional, or Ultimate can create a homegroup. Before you start the configuration, you will need two or more computers running Windows 8 or Windows 8.1. To create a homegroup, follow these steps:

1. Click Search on the Charms bar, type Control Panel, and click Control Panel from the list below.
2. Click Network and Internet, and click Choose homegroup and sharing options.
3. Click on one of the following two options (see Figure 27):
   a. If you have not created a homegroup, click Create a homegroup.
   b. If you already have a homegroup, you can change homegroup settings or join an existing homegroup.
4. Click Next, select the items you want to share with other computers running Windows, and then click Next again.
5. Click Save changes, write down the assigned password, and click Finish.
6. Open HomeGroup from the Control Panel on each of the computers to be connected, and click Join. Select the files and devices that you want to share with other homegroup members, click Next, and type the password to access the shared files and devices.
7. Once your computer network is connected and included in a homegroup, use the Homegroup folder to access shared files and printers. To go to the homegroup, open File Explorer, and click Homegroup in the Navigation pane on the left. Under HomeGroup in the left pane, navigate to the computer and files or resources that you want to access.

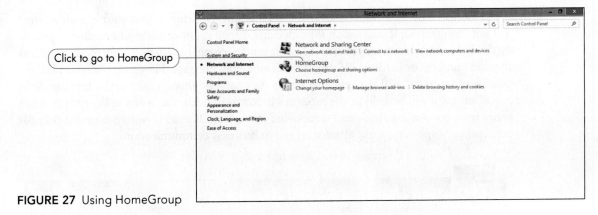

FIGURE 27 Using HomeGroup

If your home network will include computers with versions of Windows other than Windows 8 or Windows 8.1, you must use the same workgroup name for all computers that were granted access to the home network. *Workgroup* is a term used by earlier Windows versions to identify a collection of shared resources (computers, printers, and other networked devices). The method of managing a workgroup is different and a little more complex than that used to create and manage a homegroup.

Electronic Communication and Collaboration

Although e-mail continues to be a primary means of electronic communication, other methods—such as instant messaging, texting, social networking, blogs (Weblogs), podcasts, and newsgroups—are also quite popular. Perhaps you have participated in teleconferences or *webinars*, which are online connections between people at different locations, where you learn a new skill or interact with a group online. You might have even shared files via the Web to collaborate on projects and write documents. In this section, you will learn about ways to communicate and collaborate over the Internet.

Communicating over the Internet

Many people find it difficult to imagine staying in touch without using the Internet. People of all ages use *e-mail* and *instant messaging (IM)* to communicate with each other. Using social networking sites, such as Facebook, Twitter, and Instagram, is a popular way to share photos and comments. *Podcasts* bring audio and video clips to your computer so that you can listen to class lectures, radio shows, and audio books. *Blogs* are journals that are posted online. You can even use a service known as *Voice over Internet Protocol (VoIP)* to use your Internet connection as a telephone to make domestic or international calls. The Internet makes it possible to connect with friends frequently and instantly.

Use E-mail

Electronic mail (or e-mail) has been a primary means of communication over the Internet for many years. E-mail is the most-often-cited means of communication among users of the Internet. The type of e-mail account you use is up to you. You might use the e-mail account provided by your ISP primarily for personal communication while reserving your work or school e-mail account for those related matters. You can also choose to create and use a Web-based e-mail account. Sites such as Outlook, Yahoo and Google allow you to create free Web-based e-mail accounts. The benefit of Web-based e-mail account is that you can access your e-mail from any computer that is connected to the Internet and also from your smartphone. Another advantage of using such an e-mail setup is that your e-mail address will not change, even if you switch ISPs. Because e-mail is not considered a secure or private method of communication, you should never send personal or sensitive information, such as account numbers or banking information, in an e-mail message. However, e-mail is ideal for quick written notes, and you can also attach files such as photographs or documents. Your e-mail message will be held in the receiver's inbox until he or she opens it; the recipient can easily reply by clicking *Reply* and composing a response. E-mail is widely used not only for personal correspondence but also for school or business communications.

 Tip Use Multiple E-Mail Accounts

Just as your home mailbox sometimes becomes crowded with junk mail, so can an electronic mailbox. Consider opening a Web-based e-mail account with a provider such as Yahoo (mail.yahoo.com) or gmail (mail.google.com). That way, you can direct all unimportant or non-personal e-mail into that account and avoid cluttering your primary e-mail account. If you plan to use the secondary e-mail account for business correspondence, be sure to create a professional user name. For example, you might select tbarnes@yahoo.com instead of girlzrule@yahoo.com.

 Tip Stay Safe Online

The Internet is a fascinating place that has much to offer. Unfortunately, you might also find things that are not so attractive, such as Internet fraud and attempts by cybercriminals (people who use the Internet to perpetrate crimes) to steal your identity. Be well informed by visiting sites such as www.onguardonline.gov to learn what to expect and how to counteract Internet offenses.

Use Blogs

A blog (short for Weblog) is an online journal. If you have access to the Internet, you can post a blog through a free blog hosting site such as LiveJournal (www.livejournal.com) or Blogger (www.blogger.com). You might wonder why you would want to post a blog. Some people enjoy recording journal entries of their travels or documenting a family experience. Others enjoy contributing to topic-specific community blogs, such as book club discussions. Some businesses use blogs for marketing purposes. For example, a local photographer could post a blog with a few sample photos from a recent photo shoot, encouraging additional business. In fact, *vlogs (video logs)* allow users to post video as well as text to many social networking sites. If your blog is personal, you might consider making it private so that only those you invite can view the content.

Use Instant Messaging

Much like a telephone conversation (except in a written format), IM enables you to communicate with others who are also online. Unlike e-mail, IM is synchronous, which means that as you send an instant message, the receiver immediately views it and is able to respond. On the other hand, an e-mail message is asynchronous, because it resides in an electronic mailbox until the receiver retrieves it. An IM service, such as ICQ, Messaging app in Windows 8 or Skype in Windows 8.1, Google Hangouts, AOL Messaging (AIM), and even Facebook, enables you to set up a list of contacts (sometimes called *friends*). When one of your contacts is also online, you can send him or her a request to talk. He or she can accept or reject the communication. You can chat online with several people in private conversations, or you can set up an IM chat room where you can all converse together. As nice as it can be to chat online through IM, there may be times when you need to complete a task uninterrupted. Many IM services offer a stealth mode that enables you to be online without notification to your IM contacts. Some IM services offer the possibility of using a microphone and webcam so that you can hear and see each other as you talk. More and more businesses are also using IM services to reach out to their customers and colleagues.

Use Voice over Internet Protocol

If you have friends or family in far-flung locations, you might enjoy using Voice over Internet Protocol (VoIP), which enables you to use your computer as a telephone. The only difference is that your voice is transmitted digitally instead of as analog transmission from a regular telephone. You will need a computer connected to the Internet, speakers, a microphone, and a VoIP provider to use the service. With the exception of Windows 8.1, most likely, you will need to install software (usually free) from a company such as Skype (www.skype.com). Many companies offer free basic services but often require a paid subscription for additional and more advanced features.

Collaborating over the Internet

You may have participated in team projects, either in class or at work, in which members all contributed to a document or an end product. If that product is generated by a computer, you might have had to find creative ways to share it while it was being developed. Thanks to online storage sites such as OneDrive, Google Drive, Dropbox, and iCloud, as well as collaborative Web sites, called *wikis*, that job is now a lot easier to accomplish. Any team member can access a document, modify it, and make it available for others to continue the development. Sharing and collaborating online is a practice that can yield immeasurable benefits and increase productivity.

Use Wikis

A wiki is a Web site that allows people to change its content. The most recognizable wiki is the Wikipedia (www.wikipedia.org), whose entries are updated continually by experts and others. Other wikis facilitate document sharing so that projects can be completed online by several people. There are possible problems with such open entry, such as users posting inaccurate content; however, an even greater possibility is that experts will contribute their knowledge to the Web content, helping to ensure that it remains, for the most part, current and accurate. You can create your own free wiki at Wikispaces (www.wikispaces.com) so that people you invite can contribute to discussions or express thoughts about certain topics. Wikis and blogs are similar in that they are two ways to communicate online; however, wiki content can be monitored and edited so that it is more indicative of group opinion and less linked to specific individuals, as is the case with blogs.

Share Documents

Collaborating online often involves sharing and editing documents. Wikis are an excellent source for collaborative writing, as are sites such as Office Online, Google Drive (docs.google.com), and Zoho Docs (www.zoho.com/docs). For instance, when using Google Drive, you can upload Microsoft Office files (or use Google's suite of productivity software) and let team members edit the files simultaneously. It will not be necessary for team members to store various versions of the working documents online or to e-mail large file attachments to each other. The team leader can also control sharing and editing privileges. Zoho also stores all files in a central location, encouraging communication, editing, and viewing of documents. Other popular online sharing sites include OneDrive and Dropbox, where you can share photos and videos with your family and friends or even work on documents with your colleagues.

Computer Security and Privacy

Computer networks enable computers to communicate and share resources, especially over the Internet. As handy as the Internet and open access to others on your network can be, that convenience brings an unwelcome risk: violation of computer security and privacy. People who intend to cause havoc will write computer viruses that travel the Internet and infect networks and computers. *Viruses* can result in small user annoyances or total destruction of data or system components. Therefore, it is important that you take precautions and protect your computer system. Just as you should not drive a car without closing the doors and buckling your seat belt, you should not travel the Internet without first ensuring your security and privacy. Recognizing that the risk exists is the first step toward securing a network to minimize the risk. Tools such as Internet security software and firewalls can assist you in that task.

You can use a combination of software tools to counteract security and privacy risks. *Antivirus software* is available to identify and remove viruses. *Antispyware software* removes spyware or prevents spyware from entry into your computer. A *firewall* prevents unauthorized access to your computer files. *Parental controls* let you protect your children and restrict or monitor the Web sites they visit.

As security software has become more effective at preventing and removing malicious software, some people have turned to psychological means to steal information. Therefore, you should not depend completely on software to keep you safe; be vigilant to guard against harmful e-mail messages that attempt to steal your identity as well. In this section, you will learn how to use Windows 8.1 Action Center, evaluate security software, and identify Internet Explorer privacy and security settings.

 Tip Protect Against Wardrivers

Wardriving is the act of driving around while using a portable computer to search for wireless networks. Equipped with a computer, an antenna, and a GPS, a wardriver can easily map the locations of wireless access points—one of which could be your home network. Once connected, a wardriver can catch a free ride on your Internet connection and explore other computers on the network. Information in shared files is accessible, as well as passwords and credit card numbers that you send out to the Internet. Steps you can take to protect against wardrivers include configuring your router not to broadcast your SSID (wireless network identifier), changing the default router password, encrypting your wireless communication, and filtering the addresses that are allowed to connect to your router. Check the user manual for your router for more information on securing your network.

Using Windows 8.1 Action Center

Previous versions of Windows operating systems have used the Security Center to handle security issues. Windows 8.1 replaces the Security Center with the *Action Center* (see Figure 28), a feature that monitors security and maintenance, informing you of recommended maintenance tasks and keeping you aware of security settings. To access the Windows 8.1 Action Center, do the following:

1. Go to Control Panel.
2. Click System and Security.
3. Click Action Center.

In the Action Center, the red items are considered important issues that should be addressed immediately. A red item might be a missing antivirus program or an antivirus program that should be updated. Yellow items are suggested tasks that are lower in priority, such as defragmenting a hard disk. When you *defrag* your hard drive, you are reducing the amount of fragmented or separated pieces of files that are stored on your hard drive. You can turn a firewall on or off in the Action Center, and you can download Windows updates (modifications designed to address a security concern or to otherwise update the operating system or application software).

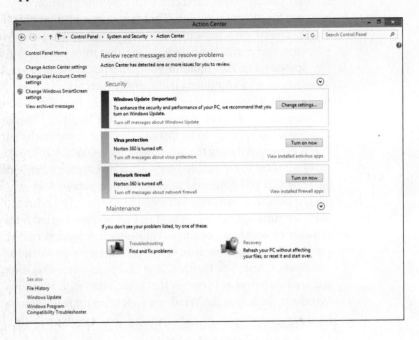

FIGURE 28 Action Center

Evaluating Security Software

Because it is very important to protect your privacy and security online, you must learn to evaluate security software. You have many choices. You can purchase antivirus software, anti-spyware software, and a firewall separately, or you can purchase all of these components in one Internet security package, such as Norton Internet Security or McAfee Internet Security. Internet Explorer incorporates several features that retain your privacy when online and others that guard against malicious Web sites and phishing attempts. As mentioned in the previous section, the Windows 8.1 Action Center works to keep you informed of security settings and available updates. For Windows 8 and prior versions, you can download the free Microsoft Security Essentials. Windows 8.1 has a beefed-up version of Windows Defender that protects your computer from viruses and malware.

Antivirus software helps protect your computer from a virus, which is a program designed to damage data or equipment or to annoy computer users. Viruses are never accidental; they are purposely written to be malicious. Most viruses travel on legitimately downloaded files or as e-mail attachments. If you keep your antivirus software current, it is unlikely that your computer system will be infected with a virus. However, there is a possibility that an unknown virus may be released before antivirus developers can respond with updates that identify and remove the code.

Some new computers come preloaded with a trial version of antivirus software. After 60 to 90 days, you must purchase the antivirus software to keep it from being disabled. Of course, you can install a different type of antivirus software if you choose. Most antivirus software is configured so that it automatically scans your computer at preset intervals, protecting you against viruses. It will also download updates (remedies for recently identified viruses) automatically if you prefer, although you can adjust the time when the updates occur so that you will not have to remember to check for current virus updates. Of course, you can run a full system scan at any time and manually check for virus fixes at the antivirus software's Web site. If you are running older antivirus software that does not automatically update itself, you will need to read the software manual or check the help files to determine how to download updated virus definitions as well as how to cause the software to constantly run in the background (reside in memory as long as the computer is on).

Spyware

Whereas viruses are designed to annoy you or cause damage to your computer or data files, *spyware* is software that has been downloaded and installed onto your computer to track your Internet travel, gather personal information, or change computer settings. At the very least, spyware usually collects and communicates information on your browsing habits to marketers who pay for that information. That way, companies are able to target you for special advertising. In a worst case, spyware might log your keystrokes so that if you type a credit card number when you purchase an item online, that information could be used to steal your identity.

Spyware can also monitor your Internet activity, reporting your preferences to Internet servers (powerful computers that manage Internet resources) that then inundate you with junk mail or hijack (redirect) your browser to marketing Web sites. Spyware most often accompanies software or files that you download from the Internet. Whether or not you realize it, you often agree to allow spyware to be installed on your computer when you accept a license agreement that is presented during the download process. Words to the effect that you agree to allow third-party software to be installed on your computer are often hidden in the fine print of a license agreement. If you download software from reputable sites, you are most often not at risk.

Antispyware software is available to identify and remove spyware. Some antispyware software runs in the background so that you are alerted if there is an attempt to change your browser or computer settings. Webroot's Spy Sweeper is an example of such software. You must purchase Spy Sweeper, but other antispyware software, such as Ad-Aware by Lavasoft and Spybot Search & Destroy, is available as a free download. Windows Defender is a full-featured antispyware program that is included with Windows 8.1 as well as earlier versions of Windows. To access the Windows Defender, do the following:

1. Open Search from the Charms bar, type Windows Defender, and click Windows Defender from the list below the search text box.
2. Click the Update tab if your virus and spyware definitions need to be updated.
3. Click the History tab to view any Quarantined items.
4. To start a scan yourself, click the Home tab, choose one of the three Scan options (Quick, Full, or Custom), and click Scan now. If possible, you should configure your antispyware software to scan your system at least once each week or manually run the scan yourself every few days.
5. Click the Settings tab to turn real-time protection on or off. You may exclude certain files or file types to be scanned. When you are done, click Save changes.

If you have been accessing the Internet for some time before installing antispyware software, you will probably be in for a surprise when you scan your computer for the first time. You might learn that there are hundreds of occurrences of spyware on your computer that can be removed. Although you should not run more than one antivirus program on your computer, you can (and probably should) run more than one antispyware program. Because antispyware software bases its spyware definitions on a built-in database, each type of software might include a slightly different database. Therefore, you might eliminate a broad range of spyware if you run more than one antispyware program.

Cookies

Some items identified by antispyware software are *cookies*. In their simplest form, cookies are not a threat to your privacy or security. In fact, they can be helpful, as they identify you as a returning visitor to a Web site, perhaps providing log-in information that you are not likely to remember from your previous visit. Along with site passwords, cookies often save shopping cart data and personalization preferences. For example, Amazon uses cookies as a marketing tool to automatically "remember" customers on return visits to display personalized recommendations. Only the Web site that created the cookie can read it, so you should not have to worry about anyone capturing your personal information via cookies.

Privacy issues arise when a Web site uses a third-party company to provide advertising. To do so, the company might use tracking cookies, which are more than simple text files. They actually track your Internet travels and display personalized advertisements based on your interests. These third-party cookies are flagged by antispyware applications. Although they pose no real danger, they do invade your privacy to a certain extent. As long as you do not provide private data by completing forms in pop-up ads, the intrusion is little more than an annoyance. Nevertheless, advertisers learn a little more about your interests, one click at a time. When these tracking cookies are flagged by your antispyware software, you can choose to delete them.

You can also choose to block third-party cookies or delete all the cookies stored on your hard drive by taking advantage of your Web browser configuration tools. Internet Explorer 11 includes a Safety tab on the Command bar (see Figure 29) that provides access to a range of safety tools. If the Command bar does not appear by default, right-click anywhere in the blank space near the URL address bar, and click *Command bar* on the list. Click the *Safety tab* on the Command bar to view a list of safety choices available to you.

FIGURE 29 Internet Explorer Safety Settings

Firewall

A firewall protects your computer from unauthorized access by *hackers*, as well as from spyware attempting to transmit your personal information to a remote location. A hacker is a person who breaks into a computer system unlawfully. A hacker could possibly steal personal information, including account numbers and passwords, from your computer. Therefore, it is imperative that you protect yourself with a firewall and that you refrain from recording any personal information in a location that could be compromised.

A firewall can be either hardware or software; for instance, the router can act as a firewall. Most home computers are protected by a personal firewall, which is software designed to secure any open avenues to your computer, in effect making your computer invisible to others. You can configure your firewall to recognize which programs on your machine should be allowed to communicate over the Internet. A firewall protects your computer both from unauthorized incoming traffic and from outgoing traffic (e.g., spyware transmissions). A bidirectional firewall is built into Windows 8.1, but you can install a separate firewall (perhaps as a component of an Internet Security package). When you install a second firewall, it will turn off the Windows 8.1 firewall so that only one firewall is active. It is not necessary to run two firewalls. If you use Windows 8.1 Firewall, you should make sure that it is turned on by checking it periodically. Access the firewall by opening the Control Panel, click System and Security, and then select Windows Firewall (see Figure 30).

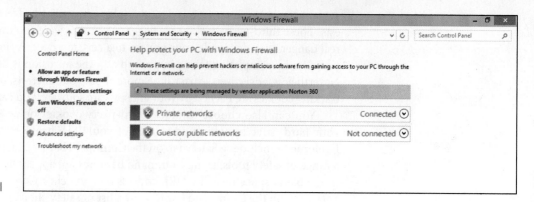

FIGURE 30 Windows Firewall

Phishing

Phishing is an e-mail scam in which the sender tries to dupe you into revealing credit card, bank account, or other personal information that could be used to steal your identity. In the e-mail, you might be instructed to click a link to visit an "official" Web site. The e-mail asks that you provide your account information, Social Security number, or other personal information so that your account can be verified. The intent is to steal your identity. These e-mails, which are usually very convincing, might contain images and text that look official, as well as links to Web sites that might appear to be legitimate sites. Watch carefully, though, for spelling errors and obvious grammatical mistakes—signs that the e-mail is not official. Be aware that legitimate companies will never ask you to provide account information through e-mail, so do not respond to any questionable e-mail. Internet Explorer includes a phishing filter, which flags known phishing sites that you might visit.

Identifying Internet Explorer Privacy and Security Settings

Internet Explorer takes your privacy and security seriously, providing several ways to keep your computer safe when you are online. Because phishing Web sites (those to which you are sometimes directed in a phishing e-mail) often deceive you into believing that you are visiting a legitimate site, Internet Explorer provides *domain highlighting*, which identifies the real Web address. A domain is a name that identifies a particular Web page. The top-level domain (the primary name that identifies the Web site's owner) is shown in black, whereas the rest of the address is grayed out (see Figure 31). *SmartScreen Filter* is a feature that helps protect you from online phishing attacks, fraud, and malicious Web sites. *InPrivate Browsing* enables you to surf the Web without leaving a history trail in the browser. When you are in private mode, an InPrivate indicator appears beside the Web address (see Figure 32). In Internet Explorer, you will also see *ActiveX Filtering*, which allows you to browse the Internet without running any ActiveX controls. Although ActiveX Filtering is disabled by default, you can easily turn it on by clicking *Safety* on the Command bar and then selecting *ActiveX Filtering*. Sometimes, ActiveX Filtering will prevent a Flash video from playing successfully in the Web browser. If you receive an error message, just disable ActiveX Filtering and the video problem will disappear. You can always turn it on again after watching the video. SmartScreen Filter, InPrivate Browsing, and ActiveX Filtering are all options available on the Internet Explorer Safety menu.

Domain highlighting

InPrivate Browsing

Click to turn off
SmartScreen Filter

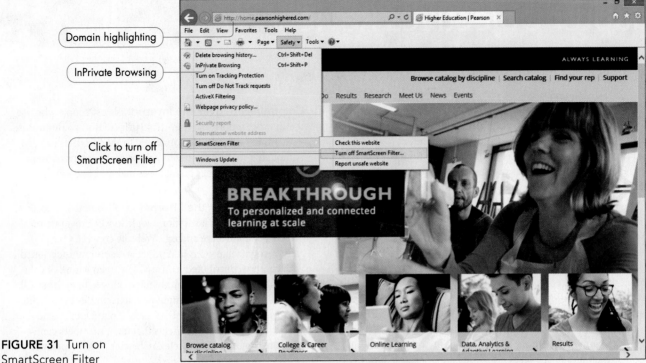

FIGURE 31 Turn on
SmartScreen Filter

InPrivate indicator

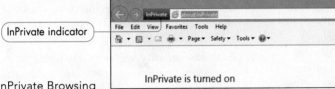

FIGURE 32 InPrivate Browsing

You can adjust privacy and security settings, delete temporary files (including cookies), and remove browsing history in your Internet Explorer so that others who use the computer will not be able to see where you have been.

Quick
Concepts

1. What are the differences between hardware and software? (*p. 2*)

2. Describe some ways that you can communicate and collaborate with others over the Internet. (*p. 25*)

3. Describe three ways to protect your computer from viruses, spyware, and cookies. (*p. 29*)

Chapter Objectives Review

After reading this chapter, you have accomplished the following objectives:

1. **Identify hardware.** Computers can be classified into different categories, ranging from supercomputers to phablets. A computer system is composed of both hardware and software. Hardware is designed to support input, processing, output, and storage functions, and includes tangible equipment such as a keyboard, mouse, webcam, microphone, monitor, printer, system unit, hard drive, and DVD.

2. **Work with software.** Software provides instructions that tell computer hardware how to accomplish specific tasks. Software can be categorized as either system software (concerned with computer-related activities such as accepting input from a keyboard and saving files to a disk) or application software (focused on specific user tasks such as word processing or gaming). System software can further be divided into the operating system and utility programs. Popular examples of application software are Microsoft Word, Excel, PowerPoint, and Access.

3. **Identify network equipment.** Computers and peripherals can be connected together via wired cables or wireless networks. Wi-Fi uses radio waves to transfer data among devices. Bluetooth uses short-range wireless connections that are usually less than 30 feet. A wired network most commonly uses Ethernet, but in some instances, phone lines or powerlines are also used.

4. **Understand transmission media.** Dial-up is the earliest, and least costly, way to connect to the Internet but offers the slowest connection. Connection types that provide faster transmissions are called broadband, and they have multiple channels in one cable or transmission path. Broadband technologies include cable, DSL, fiber optics, and satellite. Depending on your speed and cost preferences, each connection offers advantages and disadvantages. Regardless of how you connect to the Internet, you will contract with an ISP, which is most often also your broadband provider, for a gateway to the Internet.

5. **Configure a home network.** If you have several computers in your home, you might want to connect them so that they can share access to the Internet or share a printer or hard disk. Windows 8.1 provides the HomeGroup feature, which coordinates computers and resources.

6. **Communicate over the Internet.** Most people who use the Internet report that they do so primarily to communicate with others who are also connected to the Internet. Although e-mail continues to be a primary means of online communication, other possibilities include blogging, IM, podcasts, social networking, and VoIP.

7. **Collaborate over the Internet.** Collaborative Web sites, such as wikis, make it easy for people to work together on projects or contribute and edit Web site content. One of the most recognizable wikis is Wikipedia, an online encyclopedia with content contributed by users. The open nature of wiki sites encourages expert commentary, outweighing the small possibility that someone might post inaccurate content. Sites such as OneDrive, Google Drive, and Zoho Docs provide locations for shared documents that team members can work with simultaneously. Projects can be completed quickly and easily by sharing them online.

8. **Use Windows 8.1 Action Center.** Windows 8.1 has a feature called Action Center that helps you monitor security and maintenance and informs you of any recommended maintenance tasks and security settings.

9. **Evaluate security software.** Your computer can acquire a virus whenever you open an e-mail attachment, download a program, or share files. Spyware that monitors your Internet travels for the purpose of collecting personal information and preferences can transmit that information to entities that target you for marketing or that redirect your browser to a marketing Web site. Phishing is an e-mail scam that attempts to steal your identity by acquiring your personal financial information or identifying numbers. Antivirus software works to rid your computer of viruses, and antispyware software removes spyware and also identifies cookies. A firewall can protect your computer from unauthorized access by hackers.

10. **Identify Internet Explorer privacy and security settings.** Internet Explorer provides safety features that minimize phishing attempts and ensure safe Internet browsing. SmartScreen Filter is a feature that helps protect you from online phishing attacks, fraud, and malicious Web sites. InPrivate Browsing enables you to surf the Web without leaving a history trail in the browser. ActiveX Filtering allows you to browse the Internet without running any ActiveX controls.

Matching Key Terms

Match the key terms with their definitions. Write the key term letter by the appropriate numbered definition.

a. Application software
b. Bluetooth
c. Blu-ray disc (BD)
d. Broadband
e. Central processing unit (CPU)
f. Cookie
g. Fiber optics
h. Firewall
i. Google Glass
j. Hacker

k. Phishing
l. Random access memory
m. Read-only memory (ROM)
n. Soft copy
o. Spyware
p. Stylus
q. Utility program
r. Virus
s. Voice over Internet Protocol (VoIP)
t. Webinars

1. _____ A software or hardware component that prevents unauthorized access to or from a computer connected to the Internet.

2. _____ Concerned with specific user tasks, such as creating documents, sending e-mail, or working with digital photographs.

3. _____ Online connections between people at different locations, where you learn a new skill or interact with a group online.

4. _____ This technology is a wireless communication that uses low-bandwidth, short-range wireless connections (usually less than 30 feet) between computers and peripherals.

5. _____ A maliciously written software program that can result in small user annoyances or total destruction of data or system components.

6. _____ A text file that is placed on a computer that identifies the user as a returning visitor to a Web site.

7. _____ Computer memory that stores data and programs that are currently in use.

8. _____ An e-mail scam in which the sender tries to dupe you into revealing credit card, bank account, or other personal information that could be used to steal your identity.

9. _____ Uses glass fibers to transmit data at the speed of light.

10. _____ A wearable computer with an optical head-mounted display.

11. _____ Enables you to use your Internet connection as a telephone to make domestic or international calls.

12. _____ A high-definition DVD format that can hold up to nine hours of high-definition video.

13. _____ Someone who gains unauthorized access to a computer system for the purpose of stealing information or performing malicious acts.

14. _____ A pen-shaped instrument used to input commands into a computer or mobile device by drawing, writing, or selecting options on the touchscreen.

15. _____ Memory built into the computer that normally can only be read but not written to.

16. _____ Software that has been downloaded and installed onto your computer to track your Internet travel, gather personal information, or change computer settings.

17. _____ A silicon chip containing the circuitry that controls all the computer's activities.

18. _____ An Internet connection that divides a transmission path into channels to accommodate more data traffic. Examples include DSL and cable.

19. _____ An application that performs special functions related to coordinating system resources and file management.

20. _____ A monitor display of text, graphics, and video that is not permanent.

Multiple Choice

1. Software that is concerned with basic computer tasks such as accepting input from the keyboard and displaying output on a monitor is called:
   - (a) Operating system.
   - (b) Utility programs.
   - (c) System software.
   - (d) Action software.

2. A router:
   - (a) Amplifies a signal so that it is more easily transmitted to all nodes on a network.
   - (b) Enables several computers to share a single Internet connection.
   - (c) Directs computer traffic from the CPU to external devices.
   - (d) Connects computers through existing power lines.

3. The Internet connection that divides existing telephone lines into channels so that you can browse the Internet without tying up the phone line is:
   - (a) DSL.
   - (b) Cable.
   - (c) Satellite.
   - (d) Dial-up.

4. E-mail that attempts to trick you into divulging personal information such as account numbers or financial data is called:
   - (a) Blogging.
   - (b) Processing.
   - (c) Phishing.
   - (d) Networking.

5. A byte is:
   - (a) A binary representation of a single character.
   - (b) The smallest binary unit possible.
   - (c) A collection of four bits.
   - (d) A collection of characters.

6. A collaborative Web site that encourages users to contribute content is a(n):
   - (a) Wiki.
   - (b) Web Share.
   - (c) Podcast.
   - (d) IM.

7. A firewall protects against which of the following security risks?
   - (a) Identity theft
   - (b) Cookies
   - (c) Unnecessary software updates
   - (d) Unauthorized access by a hacker

8. Which of the following is a type of high-density optical storage capable of holding up to nine hours of high-definition video?
   - (a) CD-RW
   - (b) DVD-RW
   - (c) DVD-ROM
   - (d) Blu-ray

9. A blog is a(n):
   - (a) Video or audio clip saved in a compressed format such as MP3.
   - (b) Social networking site.
   - (c) Online journal.
   - (d) Web site that facilitates document sharing.

10. A slight disadvantage of a cable Internet connection is that it is:
    - (a) Slow compared with other broadband technologies.
    - (b) Shared with neighbors so speed might decrease during peak usage times.
    - (c) Not possible to bundle cable Internet with television and telephone services.
    - (d) Slower than dial-up connection.

11. Which display technology provides higher contrast and better viewing angles?
    - (a) LCD
    - (b) LED
    - (c) OLED
    - (d) CRT

12. Output that is displayed on a monitor is known as:
    - (a) Temporary copy.
    - (b) Virtual copy.
    - (c) Soft copy.
    - (d) Permanent copy.

13. Which type of drive is connected to a computer through a USB port and is most often used to transport files between computers?

   (a) Hard disk

   (b) Expansion card

   (c) Flash drive

   (d) Blu-ray

14. Which of the following acts as the brain of a computer, directing traffic and interpreting program instructions?

   (a) Motherboard

   (b) CPU

   (c) Network adapter

   (d) ROM

15. Because the contents of RAM are dependent upon a steady supply of power, it is described as:

   (a) Volatile.

   (b) Tentative.

   (c) Read-only.

   (d) Secondary.

End-of-Chapter Exercises

1 Finding Your System Specifications

This exercise requires that you locate and review your computer specifications (also called specs). Perform the following steps:

a. Open **Search** on the Charms bar, type **Control Panel**, and click **Control Panel** from the list below the search box.

b. Click **System and Security** and then click **System**.

c. Determine the following specifications for your computer. Open a blank Word document to tabulate your specs information.

- PC name
- Product ID (e.g., 00261-80173-28511-AA104)
- Type and speed of processor (e.g., Intel® Core™ i5-2520M CPU @ 2.50GHz).
- Amount of installed memory (RAM) (e.g., 4.00 GB, 3.88 GB usable).
- System type (e.g., 32- or 64-bit operating system, x64-based processor).
- Pen and touch (e.g., No pen or touch input is available for this display).
- Version of windows that you have (e.g., Windows 8.1 Pro).

d. Open **Search** on the Charms bar, type **Snip**, and click **Snipping Tool** from the list below the search box. Click **New** and drag a rectangle around the System window to copy it to the clipboard.

e. Click below the specification text in the Word document and then click **Paste** to place a copy of the snip in the document.

f. Save the file as **Concepts_Solution1_LastFirst**.

g. Exit Word and close all open dialog boxes and windows. You do not have to save the snip as a file.

h. Submit the Word document to your instructor as directed.

2 Exploring Internet Explorer

In this chapter, you learned how to keep your computer safe using the privacy and security settings in Internet Explorer. In this exercise, you will explore more about the filtering options—SmartScreen Filter, InPrivate Browsing, and ActiveX Filtering—by performing the following steps:

a. Open Internet Explorer, and type your college's Web site URL into the address bar.

b. Click **Safety** on the Command bar.

> **TROUBLESHOOTING:** If you do not see the Command bar or Safety button, right-click on the bar at the top of the window and then click **Command bar**.

c. Explore each of the safety settings, and observe the effects of each setting or change as described in the chapter materials.

d. Open **Search** on the Charms bar, type **Snip**, and click **Snipping Tool** from the list below the search box. Click **New**. Use the Snipping Tool to capture three separate screenshots of the three settings—SmartScreen Filter, InPrivate Browsing, and ActiveX Filtering.

e. Paste all three images onto a Word document.

f. Save the Word document as **Concepts_Solution2_LastFirst**.

g. Exit Internet Explorer and close any open windows.

h. Submit the Word document to your instructor as directed.

3 | Understanding Computer System Performance

Do you know that you can measure your system's performance by using the Task Manager tool in Windows? To do this, perform the following steps:

a. Press Ctrl+Alt+Delete and click **Task Manager**.

b. Click the various tabs in the dialog box to review the various features—Processes, Performance, App history, Startup, Users, Details, and Services.

> **TROUBLESHOOTING:** If you do not see tabs in the Task Manager window, click **More Details** at the bottom of the window.

c. Click the **Performance tab**.

d. Open **Search** on the Charms bar, type **Snip**, and click **Snipping Tool** from the list below the search box. Click **New**. Use the Snipping Tool to capture a screenshot of one of the charts measuring the performance of any of the following components: CPU, Memory, Disk, Bluetooth, Mobile, Ethernet, or Wi-Fi.

e. Copy and paste the screenshot onto a Word document.

f. Write a paragraph on your observations in the Word document.

g. Save the Word file as **Concepts_Solution3_LastFirst**.

h. Close the Task Manager window, but keep the Word document open for the following steps.

You will test the network speed of your computer connection by performing the following steps:

i. Launch Internet Explorer.

j. Type www.speedtest.net in the address bar.

k. Click **Begin Test** once the page loads. Observe and record the results in a Word document. It will take a few moments for your network speed to be generated.

l. Use the Snipping Tool to capture a screenshot of the results.

m. Copy and paste the screenshot onto the Word document.

n. Write a paragraph on your observations in the Word document. Click **Save**.

o. Exit Word and close all open windows.

p. Submit the document to your instructor as directed.

4 | Reviewing Computer's Status and Improving System Performance

After using your computer for a while, you realize that your system is performing too slowly. There are several things you can do to improve the performance of your computer. For instance, you can (1) review your computer's status and resolve some of the issues; (2) perform a disk cleanup to free up some space; (3) set monthly schedule to optimize your hard drive; and (4) make sure that your system is set up to receive automatic updates. Perform the following steps for this exercise:

Review your computer's status and resolve issues

a. Open **Search** on the Charms bar, type **Control Panel**, and click **Control Panel** from the list below the search box.

b. Click **System and Security** and click **Action Center**.

c. Review your computer's status and resolve any issues as needed.

d. Open **Search** on the Charms bar, type **Snip**, and click **Snipping Tool** from the list below the search box. Click **New**. Use the Snipping Tool to capture a screenshot of your maintenance items, and paste the snips into a Word document.

e. Save the Word document as **Concepts_Solution4_LastFirst**. Leave the document open for the following steps.

Perform disk cleanup

f. Open File Explorer.

g. Right-click **Local Disk (C:)** under Computer in the Navigation pane. Click **Properties**.

h. Click the **Compress this drive to save disk space check box**.

i. Click **Disk Cleanup** in the Local Disk (C:) Properties dialog box.

j. Select all the check boxes in the Disk Cleanup for (C:) dialog box, and click **OK**.

k. Click **Delete Files** in the Disk Cleanup dialog box.

l. Use the Snipping Tool to capture several screenshots of the Properties and Cleanup dialog boxes, and paste the snip into the **Concepts_Solution4_LastFirst** Word document. Click **Save**.

m. Close File Explorer. Leave the Word document open for the following steps.

Set monthly schedule to optimize your hard drive

n. Open **Search** on the Charms bar, type **Control Panel**, and click **Control Panel** from the list below the search box.

o. Click **System and Security**, click **Administrative Tools** (scroll down if needed), then click **Defragment and optimize your drives**. This option will allow you to optimize all your drives to run automatically on a schedule.

p. Make sure that the hard drive (C:) is selected. Click **Change settings** in the Optimize Drives dialog box to change the Weekly default setting to Monthly.

> **TROUBLESHOOTING:** You need administrator credentials to run the Optimize Drives program. If you do not have an administrator password, click **No** to return to the Optimize Drives window.

q. Use the Snipping Tool to capture a screenshot of the Optimize Drives dialog box (with Monthly option selected), and paste the snip into the **Concepts_Solution4_LastFirst** Word document and click **Save**.

r. Close the Optimize Drives and Advanced Tools windows. Leave the Word document open for the following steps.

Make sure that your system is set up to receive automatic updates

s. Open **Search** on the Charms bar, type **Control Panel**, and click **Control Panel** from the list below the search box.

t. Click **System and Security**.

u. Click **Windows Update**. Make sure that your computer is set to automatically install updates. If not, click **Change Settings**, open the drop-down under Important updates, click **Install updates automatically (recommended)**, and then click **OK**.

v. Use the Snipping Tool to capture a screenshot of the Windows Update window, and paste the snip into the **Concepts_Solution4_LastFirst** Word document. Click **Save**.

w. Close the Windows Update window. Exit Word. Submit the document to your instructor as directed.

5 Deleting Temporary Files

When you visit a Web site or download a file from the Internet, these files are stored on your computer as temporary files. Over a period of time, these temp files can take up lots of extra space on your hard drive. Therefore, you need to periodically delete temporary files from your hard drive.

For this exercise, you will perform the following steps:

a. Complete Internet research to investigate ways that temporary files are created automatically on your system.

b. Complete Internet research to find instructions on how to locate all the directories on your computer where temporary files might reside.

c. Using Word, write a step-by-step procedure on how to delete temporary files from at least two locations on your computer. Save the file as **Concepts_Solution5_LastFirst**.

d. To delete the temporary files in Internet Explorer, open the Search menu from the Charms bar, type **Snip**, and click **Snipping Tool** from the Apps list. Click **New**. Capture a screenshot of the window using the Snipping Tool and paste it into the **Concepts_Solution5_LastFirst** Word document. Click **Save**.

e. Exit Word. Close any open windows.

f. Submit the document to your instructor as directed.

Glossary

Action Center Action Center helps you monitor security and maintenance and informs you of any recommended maintenance tasks and security settings.

ActiveX Filtering ActiveX Filtering allows you to browse the Internet without running any ActiveX controls.

all-in-one desktop All-in-one desktop computer integrates the system unit into a thin and flat-panel monitor, equipped with a high-speed wireless keyboard and mouse.

application software Application software is concerned with specific user tasks, such as creating documents, sending e-mail, or working with digital photographs.

bandwidth Bandwidth is the maximum speed that you can send or receive data over the Internet.

binary The binary system is a two-state system in which circuits must be either "on" or "off."

binary digit (bit) A binary digit (bit) has two possible values: 0s and 1s.

blog A blog (Weblog) is an online journal.

Bluetooth Bluetooth technology is wireless communication that uses low-bandwidth, short-range wireless connections (usually less than 30 feet) between computers and peripherals.

Blu-ray disc (BD) Blu-ray disc (BD) is a high-definition DVD format that can hold up to nine hours of high-definition video.

broadband A broadband connection is an Internet connection that divides a transmission path into channels to accommodate more data traffic. Examples include DSL and cable.

broadband over power line (BPL) Broadband over power line uses electrical wiring to send information between computers.

byte A byte is a binary representation of one character.

cable Cable connection is a popular broadband connection using the same technology as cable television.

CD A CD is an optical storage medium.

central processing unit (CPU) The central processing unit (CPU) is a silicon chip containing the circuitry that controls all the computer's activities.

commercial software Commercial software is software that you are not allowed to copy.

cookie A cookie is a text file that is placed on a computer that identifies the user as a returning visitor to a Web site.

copyleft Copyleft is a license agreement that comes with freeware, encouraging the user to adapt and redistribute the software and not restrict future copying.

data Data are facts that are used to produce usable results (information).

defrag Defrag is the process of reducing the amount of fragmented or separated pieces of files that are stored on the hard drive.

desktop computer A desktop computer (also commonly known as a personal computer or PC) is a computer consisting of a separate system unit, monitor, keyboard, and mouse components, typically used in a small business/home situation, and not intended for portability.

dial-up Dial-up is a very slow Internet connection that uses existing telephone lines.

digital camera A digital camera collects pictures and video data.

digital subscriber line (DSL) A digital subscriber line (DSL) is a popular broadband connection that divides existing telephone lines into several channels.

downstream Downstream speed refers to the speed for downloading data.

drive bay A drive bay is an area of space reserved in a system unit where additional disk drives such as CD or DVD drives can be installed.

DVD A DVD is an optical storage medium that has more storage capacity than a CD.

e-mail E-mail is a form of electronic communication sent over the Internet.

embedded system An embedded system is a lesser-known category of computer that is developed to perform some specific task.

Ethernet network An Ethernet network is based on the Ethernet protocol, which is a set of specifications for wired electronic data transmission.

expansion card An expansion card is a circuit board that can be connected to the motherboard to give the computer added capabilities.

external disk drive An external disk drive is a portable storage device that can be connected to a computer through a port such as a USB port.

fiber optics Fiber optics uses glass fibers to transmit data at the speed of light.

firewall A firewall is software or hardware that prevents unauthorized access to or from a computer connected to the Internet.

firmware Firmware is memory built into the computer that normally can only be read but not written to. Also see *RAM*.

flash drive A flash drive or USB drive is a small, portable flash memory device that connects to a computer's USB port.

flash memory Flash memory provides portable storage because it is an external device.

gigahertz Gigahertz (GHz) is a measurement (billions of hertz or electrical vibrations per second) used to represent processor speed.

Google Glass Google Glass is a wearable computer with an optical head-mounted display.

hacker A hacker is someone who gains unauthorized access to a computer system for the purpose of stealing information or performing malicious acts.

hard copy Hard copy is a printed output produced by a printer.

hard drive The hard drive is the primary storage unit of a computer.

hardware Hardware comprises of tangible pieces of equipment, such as a computer monitor, printer, mouse, and keyboard.

HomeGroup HomeGroup is a feature in the Windows operating system that allows all computers in the home network to access shared files.

hub A hub amplifies data transmission to all connected equipment.

information Information is data that has been organized so that it is usable.

inkjet printer An inkjet printer produces high-quality color graphics and documents at an affordable price.

InPrivate Browsing InPrivate Browsing enables you to surf the Web without leaving a history trail in the browser.

instant messaging (IM) Instant messaging (IM) enables you to communicate with your friends or colleagues online. Unlike e-mail, IM is synchronous, which means that as you send an instant message, the receiver immediately views it and is able to respond.

Internet The Internet is the world's largest network, connecting millions of computers and users around the globe.

keyboard A keyboard is a device used to enter data and commands by pressing keys.

laptop A laptop (also called a notebook) is a self-contained unit, with the monitor, keyboard, system unit, and pointing device all encased together.

laser printer Laser printers are increasing in popularity for both home and business users and are typically less costly than inkjet printers to operate.

light-emitting diode (LED) A light-emitting diode (LED) monitor can provide a more responsive display because the backlights in LED monitor are brighter than the fluorescent lamps in LCDs.

liquid crystal display (LCD) A liquid crystal display (LCD) is a flat-panel computer display.

mainframe A mainframe computer is a large, fast, and powerful computer system, but smaller than a supercomputer.

megabits per second (Mbps) Megabits per second (Mbps) refers to the upstream and downsteam speeds.

memory card A memory card or flash card is another form of a flash memory data storage device used to store digital information. They are commonly used in digital cameras, mobile phones, laptop computers, MP3 players and video game consoles.

microphone A microphone converts sound waves to a digital format for storage on or manipulation by a computer.

midrange computer A midrange computer is smaller, less powerful, and less expensive than most large mainframe computer systems, but larger, more powerful, and more expensive than most microcomputers. It is usually used as a server.

mobile computer A mobile computer is a smaller computer equipped with hardware, software, and communication capabilities to support mobile computing.

mobile operating system A mobile operating system, also referred to as mobile OS, combines the features of a personal computer operating system with other features.

monitor A monitor is an output device that displays text, graphics, and video.

motherboard The motherboard is the main circuit board of a computer located in the system unit.

mouse A mouse is a small, handheld device that enables you to execute commands, make selections, and open shortcut menus.

multifunction printer A multifunction printer offers the ability to print, scan, copy, and fax—all from one unit.

netbook A netbook is slightly smaller and lighter than a notebook.

network A network makes it possible for computers to interact with one another, sharing files and resources.

network interface card (NIC) A network interface card (NIC) is a device that is housed inside the computer on the motherboard.

node A node is a computer or another device, such as a printer, that is connected in a network.

notebook A notebook (also called a laptop) is a self-contained unit, with the monitor, keyboard, system unit, and pointing device all encased together.

operating system An operating system is a program that allows you to enter data, display text on a monitor, save files to a disk, and print documents.

optical mouse An optical mouse uses a sensor to detect mouse movement, resulting in a corresponding movement of the mouse pointer on the monitor.

organic light-emitting diode (OLED) An organic light-emitting diode (OLED) is a newer technology than LCD and LED that provides higher contrast and better viewing angles because it works without a backlight.

parental control Parental controls let you protect your children and restrict or monitor the Web sites they visit.

phablet A phablet is a hybrid between a smartphone and a mini tablet, frequently with a display screen greater than 5 inches.

phishing Phishing is an e-mail scam in which the sender tries to dupe you into revealing credit card, bank account, or other personal information that could be used to steal your identity.

podcast A podcast brings audio and video clips to your computer so that you can listen to class lectures, radio shows, and audio books.

printer A printer is capable of creating paper or hard copy output of both text and color graphics.

productivity software Productivity software is a category of application software that enables you to accomplish tasks such as writing a word document, balancing a spreadsheet, or creating a slide presentation.

random access memory (RAM) Random access memory (RAM) is computer memory that stores data and programs that are currently in use.

read-only memory (ROM) Read-only memory (ROM) is memory built into the computer that normally can only be read but not written to.

resolution The resolution is the number of pixels (tiny dots of light, also called picture elements) that are displayed on a monitor. Image size is often referred to in pixels.

router A router is a device that connects to an Internet modem, enabling several computers to share an Internet connection.

satellite Satellite Internet connection uses satellites to broadcast data.

scanner A scanner is used to convert existing pictures or text into digital format and send those images to a computer for manipulation and printing.

shareware Shareware is software that is available for free trial so that you can download and use before purchasing it with a voluntary payment.

SmartScreen Filter SmartScreen Filter is a feature that helps protect you from online phishing attacks, fraud, and malicious Web sites.

soft copy Soft copy is a monitor display of text, graphics, and video that is not permanent.

software Software is a set of instructions that tells a computer what to do.

solid state drive (SSD) A solid state drive (SSD) is a primary storage medium residing inside the computer that is built around semiconductors and chips rather than a magnetic media such as the traditional hard drive.

sound card A sound card is a component that enables a computer to work with sound.

speaker A speaker is an output device that produces sound.

spyware Spyware is software that has been downloaded and installed onto your computer to track your Internet travel, gather personal information, or change computer settings.

stylus A stylus is a pen-shaped instrument used to input commands to a computer screen or mobile device by drawing, writing, or selecting options on the touchscreen.

supercomputer Supercomputers are the most powerful systems in the world.

switch A switch is a device that directs traffic along a wired network.

system software System software coordinates communication between the application software and computer hardware.

system unit The system unit is the main component of a computer system, containing the processor, memory, and storage devices.

tablet A tablet is a mobile computer that is available in various sizes.

thrashing Thrashing occurs when excessive paging operations take place.

touchpad A touchpad is a touch-sensitive pad built into the keyboard of a laptop or notebook.

trackpoint A trackpoint is a button that you move with your finger to position a mouse pointer on the screen.

upstream Upstream speed refers to the speed for uploading data.

USB drive A USB drive is a small, portable flash memory device that connects to a computer's USB port.

USB port A USB port is a computer connection for devices such as keyboards, scanners, digital cameras, and microphones.

utility program A utility program is an application that performs special functions related to coordinating system resources and file management.

video card A video card (video adapter) is a component that provides display capabilities.

virus A virus is a maliciously written software program that can result in small user annoyances or total destruction of data or system components.

vlog (video log) A vlog (video log) is an online journal that uses video as the primary content in addition to text.

Voice over Internet Protocol (VoIP) Voice over Internet Protocol (VoIP) enables you to use your Internet connection as a telephone to make domestic or international calls.

webcam A webcam broadcasts pictures and video data.

webinar A webinar is an online connection between people at different locations, where you learn a new skill or interact with a group online.

Wi-Fi hotspot Wi-Fi hotspot is a wireless Internet access point.

wiki A wiki is a collaborative Web site that enables anyone to edit, delete, or modify the content.

wireless access point (WAP) A wireless access point (WAP) is a device that provides a location for wireless units to connect.

wireless fidelity (Wi-Fi) Wireless fidelity (Wi-Fi) uses radio waves to provide network and Internet connections.

wireless network A wireless network uses radio waves to communicate between devices.

wireless network adapter A wireless network adapter is a device that is required on each node of a wireless network to transmit data.

wireless printer A wireless printer is often used to print from a handheld device such as a smartphone, a notebook computer, or a digital camera.

Index

Credits